POLITICAL
PHILOSOPHY

3

POLITICAL PHILOSOPHY

3

From the Rights of Man to the Republican Idea

LUC FERRY

AND

ALAIN RENAUT

Translated by Franklin Philip

THE UNIVERSITY OF CHICAGO PRESS • CHICAGO & LONDON

Luc Ferry is professor at the Sorbonne
and at the University of Caen.

Alain Renaut teaches history of philosophy and
political philosophy at the University of Nantes.

The University of Chicago Press, Chicago 60637
The University of Chicago Press, Ltd., London

© 1992 by The University of Chicago
All rights reserved. Published 1992
Printed in the United States of America

01 00 99 98 97 96 95 94 93 92   5 4 3 2 1

Originally published as
*Philosophie politique, vol. 3:
Des droits de l'homme à l'idée républicaine.*
© Presses Universitaires de France, 1985.

Library of Congress Cataloging-in-Publication Data

Ferry, Luc.
   [Des droits de l'homme à l'idée républicaine. English]
   From the rights of man to the republican idea / Luc Ferry and
Alain Renaut.
      p.   cm.—(Political philosophy ; 3)
   Translation of: Des droits de l'homme à l'dée républicaine.
   Includes index.
   ISBN 0-226-24473-3
   1. Human rights.   I. Renaut, Alain.   II. Title.   III. Series:
Ferry, Luc. Philosophie politique ; 3.
JC571.F45413   1992
323—dc20   91-43341
                                                                    CIP

⊗The paper used in this publication meets the minimum requirements
of the American National Standard for Information Sciences—Permanence of Paper
for Printed Library Materials,
ANSI Z39.48-1984.

CONTENTS

ABBREVIATIONS

C   Pierre-Joseph Proudhon. *Correspondance de Proudhon.* 10 vols. Paris, 1875.

DF   François Guizot. *De la démocratie en France.* Paris: V. Masson, 1849.

GIR   Pierre-Joseph Proudhon. *General Idea of Revolution in the Nineteenth Century.* New York: Haskell House, 1969. *Idée générale de la révolution au XIXe siècle.* Paris: Garnier Frères, 1851.

IR   Claude Nicolet. *L'Idée républicaine en France: Essai d'histoire critique.* Paris: Gallimard, 1982.

LLL   F. A. Hayek, *Law, Legislation and Liberty: A New Statement of the Liberal Principles of Justice and Political Economy.* 3 vols. Chicago: University of Chicago Press, 1979.

NRH Leo Strauss. *Natural Right and History.* Chicago: University of Chicago Press, 1953.

OC   Pierre-Joseph Proudhon. *Oeuvres complètes.* 15 vols. Paris: M. Rivière, 1923–59.

SC   Jean-Jacques Rousseau. *The Social Contract.* New York: Hafner, 1947.

INTRODUCTION

Democracy and Human Rights

1. The Return of Human Rights?

Human rights keep falling on hard times.

True, the past few years have seen a return to those values that had been in decline during a century dominated by Marxist ideology. Signs exist, however, that this return movement is bogging down and that, despite ritualized observances and published hype, the idea of human rights risks being once again shelved with a number of other outworn accessories.

To see the logic, if a logic there is, in this recent history of an idea, we should recall the evolution in the late 1970s, promoted by journals such as *Esprit* and *Libre,* of thinking about the antitotalitarian significance of references to human rights. A discussion organized by the journal *Esprit* on the theme "Do human rights constitute a form of politics?" resulted in several publications, notably articles by Marcel Gauchet,[1] Claude Lefort,[2] and Paul Thibaud,[3] setting forth the framework for a debate. We can now make out two distinct stages in this debate about the reactivation of the reference to human rights:

(1) First, a consensus reemerged, particularly from the discussion of the Polish workers' movement and its gains during the summer and fall of 1980, to see the reference to human rights as a legitimate component of efforts for reform and freedom. To declare oneself "for" human rights and "against" their transgression became customary again, whereas, previously, the vulgate of Marxist criticism of rights as simply a formalist fiction designed to guarantee and to mask the realities of exploitation called for derision and demystification of the principles of 1789. Claude Lefort has made a large contribution to legitimating the claims of this renewed consensus by showing how, contrary to the reading of the declarations that Marx presented in *The Jewish Question,* the discourse of human rights is

1

not reducible to the workings of "bourgeois society" and how such rights "prove constitutive of democratic social space."[4] Stripped of the ideological dimension to which Marx thought the declarations were reducible, the text recovered its original sense and was given back its initial purpose: the defense of the individual against the state—thereby conclusively establishing the practical antitotalitarian impact of the reference to human rights.[5]

Even in this first phase, however, there were those who had some reservations and who emphasized that this reference, whose emancipative legitimacy was no longer in question, could not *by itself* be the key to solving the political problem presented by "the collapse of the plan for a society forged in the course of a century and a half of the worker's movement." "Human rights is not a political program"[6]—a gentle but firm warning against the tendency to consider an appeal to the "noble principles" of 1789 as an alternative to totalitarianism. A clear line of reasoning: merely because the theme of human rights legitimately and effectively serves as a brake on the state absorbing society, does not imply that the problem is thus solved of what a society freed from the threat of totalitarianism can and must be; for "a certain way of putting forward human rights indirectly amounts to legitimating the established Western order" by intimating that the rejection of communism and fascism will resolve all problems—when in fact the problems have not even been properly put: problems of injustice, inequality, alienation—in short, "nothing is decided about the social problem that occupies us."

Even if the discourse of human rights were an effective obstacle to totalitarianism, we would still need to address "the question of a just, equal, and free society." Isn't the rhetoric of human rights on this question, historically originating in the *individualistic* tradition of modern natural law in its effort to form the community starting with and founding itself on the individual—bound by definition to run into serious difficulties when it addresses the properly *political* problem, that of organizing a *collectivity* with the implied recognition of some necessary and at least partial negation of the personal sovereignty of *individuals?* In other words—and this was the main question in this article of Gauchet's—when we make the proclamation of the rights of the individual the be-all and end-all of political discourse, aren't we doomed to despair of the body politic, thus viewed as the scene of an inevitable and fatal alienation. Aren't we bound to be forever denouncing, with Hegel, beautiful spirit or (much the same thing) an unhappy consciousness, the "radical evil" inherent in the very nature of collective life? The warning was thus clearly formulated, even if one could envision other possible results of the confusion between human rights and politics. Such a use of the principles of 1789 could turn against the principles themselves: in the attempt to create a political system out of their affirmation, aren't we ourselves soon condemned—in view of the observation that they provide no leverage to deal with the concrete problems of collective organization—to denounce once again the inadequacy of the theme of human rights and in short order to relegate it to the scrap heap of bygone instruments of political debate? Thus, the way the reference to human rights was most often practiced in this first phase of their recent rehabilitation contained within it the risk of an abrupt reversal: not just fatigue but also disillusionment.

(2) As everyone knows, history never takes a holiday, and the signs of a second phase clearly started to appear in the discussion fueled, beginning in December 1981, by the setback to the Polish workers' movement. Shouldn't a course of action that was valid in 1980—when the example of Solidarity suggested the possibility of a "reconstructed social autonomy" based on the reference to human rights—already be reconsidered when one concludes, as P. Thibaud thought we must in March 1983, that the "expectations" raised by the various movements for the "conquest of new rights" were "never fulfilled"?[7] Thus there are signs of a new criticism of the discourse of human rights that is curiously reminiscent of certain points made in *The Jewish Question,* where the ineffectiveness of this discourse is attributed to a "too abstract an idea" of man and his rights.

In fact, this reversal was largely foreseeable. To be persuaded of this, we need only reflect on the illusions that gave rise to the "hopes" that were thus "dashed." P. Thibaud readily recognizes it: "At the time we published the issue "Droit et politique" [Rights and politics], *Esprit* (March 1980), it seemed to us that a new approach to politics based on the reference to human rights had been introduced." And, indeed, in the March 1980 issue one could read that "starting with human rights one can establish something other than a protest: a practical politics," in short, that "human rights can inspire a politics."[8] Three years later, we note that "human rights are used in a purely individualistic and largely apolitical acceptation," that they ground the claims that modern passive citizens make on their state instead of fostering a society's reflection about its institutions and norms"; it is concluded that the reference to human rights allows only for opposing the state with a "list of grievances" but does not really yield the means for "inventing politics."

This is no surprise. There is inherent in the discourse of human rights "a universal located outside history." If you call on Péguy for help against the "Kantians" who "remind us that a minimum of abstract humanism is needed to think of human rights," you end up detecting the symptom of "abstract universalism" in their position, an abstract universalism by definition unable to penetrate the richness and complexity of the real.[9] Starting with this "sterile and theoretical" affirmation of universal principles, the "debate" would then have to move once again toward that "work ... of self-definition to which democratic societies are destined," and for this individualistic and apolitical work the reference to human rights would be definitely too summary. So be it, but this disappointment concerning demands for reform based on the concept of human rights is clearly in proportion to the prior illusion that the demand could possibly *suffice* to make the invention of politics possible.

It is assuredly progress to determine that morality, rights, and politics are different domains—and thus, as M. Gauchet stressed three years earlier, "human rights are not a politics"; to infer from this, however, that the debate about the "too abstract" principles of law and rights opens up fewer prospects than "three years earlier," is to commit two errors:

—A theoretical error: this assumes that we take the traditional affirmation of human rights to be a claim to constitute a politics all by itself—and later it is easy to be disappointed by these claims' impotence to "invent politics," and then to call for a new stage in the debate. Rather, shouldn't we first analyze the confusion, which has not been truly avoided, between the affirmation of the principles of law [*le droit*] and the definition of a politics and the theoretical error expressed by this confusion?

—A strategic error: because of the relative pessimism this confusion produces about the impact of the affirmation of human rights, one paradoxically retreats to positions close to the ritualistic Marxist and neoconservative attacks on human rights as "abstract" or simply "formal" rights.[10] Why can't we see that one thus contributes to revitalizing a position that, by condemning the affirmation of juridical humanism as an ineffectual abstraction, risks getting trapped, like Marx, in ideology, or in other words, allowing itself "to become the prisoner of the ideological version of rights, without examining what they mean in practice, what profound changes they bring to social life"?[11]

A second return to the rights of man thus seems called for, perhaps less enthusiastic than the one that began the 1980s but that risks falling pathetically short, but this time more heedful of the true status and impact of their affirmation. Today, the point is not simply to come out once again "for" human rights: no one now dreams of going back on the reemerging consensus about the reference to these principles—even though certain worries or disappointments occur about the strictly political impact of the rhetoric of human rights. On the other hand, we need to question the very *object* of this consensus: for if we don't make the reference to human rights the subject of a *question,* the risk is great of seeing this movement once again get stuck in ideology or even—in a gesture we have just had a hint of—more or less repudiate itself. From this point of view a *philosophical* inquiry—one concerning the bases or conditions of possibility for some particular position—could seem to us not only *philosophically* legitimate with respect to this reactivation of juridical humanism (if philosophizing has something to do with thinking of what is), but also *politically necessary* if it is acknowledged that contemporary history has too often provided the spectacle of emancipatory projects aborting or even turning into their opposite for us, this time, not to spare ourselves the time for reflection.

2. Human Rights and Democratic Values: Consensus or Dissensus?

To question the very object of consensus seemingly expressed by the recovered reference to human rights is first to wonder about what the consensus is and how broad it is. In fact, things are not as clear and simple in this matter as might be thought. A public-opinion poll done by SOFRES (a private French public-opinion organization) in March 1983 to determine "the unity and diversity of the French people" calls for a good deal of discussion about the state of democratic values—supposed to express and enrich the heritage of the Declarations of the Rights of Man. Faced with the results of this poll, political columnist Alain Duhamel thought he detected the image of a "striking consensus in France," [12] particularly noticeable through the way in which the French people "proclaim themselves massively attached to every one of their rights": weren't 70 percent of the people polled agreed in considering "serious," for example, a possible suppression of the freedom to unionize? Upon closer inspection, however, the picture becomes less idyllic, to the point that, rereading the results of one study, Professor Olivier Duhamel finds, contrary to his homonymic, a perfect expression of the "French dissensus."[13] We make three observations about this rereading.

(1) Where, considering only the overall majority figures, one can get an impression of consensus,[14] the state of opinion appears in quite a different light when we note the responses of various groups of political supporters; thus in the same example we note that the support of unions is distributed very differently as we consider the support of the Gaullist Rassemblement pour la République (59 percent), the centrist Union pour la Démocratie Française (61 percent), the Socialist party (82 percent), and the Communist party (90 percent)—and that to consider a social and professional category such as store owners, the responses that the suppression of unions would be "serious" (even including the opinions going from "very serious" to "rather serious") comprise no more than 46 percent of the persons polled. The apparent consensus thus conceals a real dissensus of surprising extent (here, up to a range of 31 points if we limit ourselves to groups of political supporters).

(2) Armed with this first observation, let us, as Olivier Duhamel invites us, pay attention less to the majority figure for the whole than to the extent or, if you will, the maximal split between the groups, and be wary of adding up answers displaying strong support ("it would be very serious to suppress") and those showing a weaker support ("it would be rather serious"); in short, let's measure the differences between groups in their responses to calling "very serious" this or that right into question. It is then clear—and this is our second observation—that *certain* democratic values are very much the object of a *broad consensus,* and in first place the *right to vote:* the consensus is broadest on the exercise of this right, the difference between the extremes reducing to 9 points (UDF, 79 percent; Communist party, 88 percent). That *certain* legal values stemming from the French Revolution are thus the area in which the different groups of the French are most clearly agreed is certainly an important fact and seems to confirm the image of a recovered consensus about the principles of 1789 and certain others added in the course of the history of human rights.[15]

(3) Nevertheless, a final observation called for by this investigation suggests greater caution and reflection: if *certain* democratic values elicit a broad consensus, *other rights* do not enlist the strong

support of all and reveal singular dissensuses concerning *other* but just as traditional democratic values. While 49 percent of those polled declared that a possible suppression of the right to strike would be very serious, the difference between the extremes here reaches 52 points (UDF, 29 percent; Socialist party, 81 percent); while 33 percent of the persons questioned declared the suppression of political parties very serious, the difference reaches 28 points (UDF, 24 percent; Communist party, 52 percent); and even concerning the freedom of the press, the difference comes to 15 points (UDF, 64 percent; RPR, 79 percent).

What is the upshot of these analyses for our concerns? Without denying the progress of consensus, we are obliged to recognize that the definition of democratic values remains an object of debate. While the right to vote, a reinterpretation[16] of the right to "take part in the formation of laws," rallied 85 percent of the French, the right to strike, the freedom to unionize, and even the existence of political parties are also, in a sense, divisive issues. Nevertheless, as a result of the history of human rights, the freedom to unionize figures in article 23 of the Universal Declaration of 1948, and though the rights to strike and to form political parties do not appear in the United Nations Declaration (the Eastern bloc opposed them),[17] the preamble to the French Constitution of 1946—the latest text in force on human rights in France[18]—makes the right to strike one of the freedoms that are "particularly necessary in our time" by which the Declaration of 1789 should be supplemented, and the first section of the Constitution of 1958 has the free existence of political parties follow logically from its proclaimed allegiance "to human rights and the principles of national sovereignty." In public opinion the state of democratic values thus lags considerably behind the legal attainments of contemporary history.

Though the definition of democratic values offers so much material for discussion on this point, some thinking is needed, hard as it might be, about the weak consistency of the idea of democracy in our political imagination. Certainly, broad agreement exists about the close linkage between "the first development of the democratic state and the establishment of human rights"[19] and about human rights as "constitutive of democracy."[20] But with *what* idea of human rights or, rather, with *what* human rights is the idea of democracy associated? If today we hold human rights to be constitutive of democracy, even while some of them divide us more than they unite us, what are we to think of the robustness of the democratic idea?

Shouldn't we first go back to the *idea* of human rights and determine according to what ambiguities this idea sometimes unites and sometimes divides? Shouldn't we first get rid of these equivocations so that we can give some real specificity to juridical humanism, in the hope not of making a political program out of human rights, but of bringing out to what idea of politics—whether we call it the *idea of a democracy* or (as we shall see) that of a *republic*—a thought-through reference to these principles can lead? As long as the democratic ideal is satisfied with a poorly mastered reference to a nebulous set of rights on which as much disagreement as convergence exists, we will continue to witness the same odd phenomenon so characteristic of our political life: on the one hand, starting despite everything from the fairly broad observable consensus about *certain* democratic values, the periodically revived hope in a vast political union, for example, the French "centrist" hope, whatever form it takes, of a "sweet dream" where political wishes sometimes install center-right Simone Veil and center-left Michel Rocard as joint prime ministers, but in other respects the repeated impotence of this centrist hope to yield any true political force—as if general agreement about the values of democracy did not rule out apparently unshrinkable distances concerning the relative importance of this or that democratic value and inevitably had to turn into discord when it comes to forming a political project on the basis of agreed-upon principles.

Let us give an "experimental" demonstration of the peculiarity of this situation. Invited by the magazine *Le Nouvel Observateur* to search for "an area of possible alliance between them,"[21] Simone Veil and Michel Rocard noted—apparently to their surprise—that their respective definitions of liberalism and socialism are symmetrically different from the purest form of these two models: stating the case against the neoliberalism of Milton Friedman, Veil defends a liberalism (in the European sense, meaning the free market) that accepts "a minimum of state intervention" while leaving "the most extensive area possible to free will and personal initiative" under the protection of law; stating the case against the "collectivizing socialism of production," Rocard defends a socialism in which the state, which "does not and cannot know how to produce," is merely "a central regulator that must give the most total autonomy to the units of production" such that "the fundamental rights of individuals and groups are recognized." Under these circumstances, it is unsurprising that the two approaches link up to make democratic pluralism in one case the "lone dogma" of liberalism and in the other the "very essence" of a socialism that follows in "the tradition of Jean Jaurès and Léon Blum." We are forced to note that nevertheless the dialogue concludes with the blunt reassertion of a difference; to the question of the possibility of their political collaboration in "regluing together the pieces of France," Veil replies that "there is no compromise possible between those who subscribe to totally different and even contradictory conceptions of society," and Rocard concludes that "the question asked us makes no sense today." The whole problem, however, is surely to determine *why* this is so. The fact remains that the proof could not be clearer that both the "right" and "left" can fully share the democratic values and basic rights protecting the autonomy of individuals—in other words, the two camps can be in perfect accord at least about what their most thoughtful representatives consider the main thing—and still remain in their positions and continue to be deeply opposed. It will be said that the issue here is one of "sensibility." Perhaps, but it's still necessary to determine what intelligible difference is being confusedly expressed by this cleavage in sensibilities—short of which, we repeat, the weak consistency of the idea of democracy (meaning its specificity is so unclear that even a reference to democracy that is fleshed out as pluralistic is not enough to make possible a "compromise" between positions that regard each other as antagonistic!) dooms the celebration of democratic values to a formal and ritualistic gesture too easily seen as devoid of genuine political meaning. A fallback into a denunciation of its formalism in the name of the requirements of actual politics, even of political realism, then appears as just about inevitable, with all the nasty effects that this new ebbing would have. So it behooves us not to dodge the question of the basis of the cleavage regarded as irreducible between positions whose histories still share the common reference to the democratic values expressed in the Declarations of the Rights of Man. If, out of principle and for clear reasons, one objects to any answer that simply accuses these values and rights of a degree of abstraction and formalism too lofty to fuel anything but a superficial agreement without real import, one is led to wonder whether it isn't the discourse of human rights itself that makes this cleavage possible. In other words, don't the democratic values expressed in this discourse display a heterogeneity such that, depending on which of the various proclaimed rights we select as truly constitutive of the democratic space (and, as we have seen, in analyzing the responses to the SOFRES poll, that we do not all subscribe identically to different democratic values), we will evaluate ourselves as belonging to one or the other of the two camps, between which it will then be hard to imagine any possible "compromise"?

3. The Fundamental Ambiguity of the Democratic Reference

What then continues to drive the opposition between the two camps even though, each side knowing how to reflect on its own tradition, each manages to reach agreement with the other about the values of pluralistic democracy? Let us state the hypothesis we believe needs testing here, notably with an analysis of the possibly peculiarly heterogeneous discourse about human rights: for reasons that will be made clear and are in fact deeply philosophical and not merely affective or historical (though they are that as well), liberalism cannot easily take into account the masses and their modern political power and integrate them in its political horizon, and socialism has great difficulty thinking of the law and of rights as being values in themselves.

Thus expressed, these affirmations obviously appear either deadly truisms or blatant absurdities; the purpose of the rest of this study is to show that a real problem exists. For the moment we shall merely provide some indication of what must seem to be a twofold and symmetrical intellectual mutilation, and possibly the root of the continuing cleavage between discourses for which democratic values are, nevertheless, a common reference.

On the side of liberalism, one cannot but be struck, in reading the current Bible of so-called neoliberal thought, by the reluctance shown by F. A. Hayek in the latest volume in his *Law, Legislation, and Liberty* series regarding the idea of democracy understood as the government of an organization through the will of the majority of its members. Hayek says: "I must frankly admit that *if* democracy is taken to mean government by the unrestricted will of the majority I am not a democrat" (*LLL*, 3:39). For the moment we shall not go into detail about Hayek's arguments, to which we return when we examine the problems posed by the liberal interpretation of popular sovereignty: here we simply note that in reading Hayek one is forced to observe that on the side of liberalism, allegiance to the democratic ideal—which certainly "must be defended"—is counterbalanced by calling into question the equivalence between democracy and government by the majority. To be more precise, in Hayek the conviction is clearly apparent that the actualization of the democratic ideal (understood as the ideal of a government with a view to the common interest) is not best guaranteed by basing political authority on the will of the greatest number, which will is indeed not necessarily subordinated to the common interest but may be an alliance, a heterogeneous multiplicity of special interests. Consequently, Hayek explicitly writes, one should have the courage to ask who are the "members" who may legitimately be considered to have "a say in the matter of leading the organization to decide the objectives it will pursue." It may be said that this elitist reservation about the power of the masses is peculiar to Hayek's extremism, which has an uncommon (to say the least) conception of the election of representatives, to wit, a choice by age ranges and according to modalities such that the average age of the representatives is fifty-two-and-a-half years (*LLL,* 3: 113ff)! Beyond a marked tendency to conflate democracy and gerontocracy, however, Hayek's thinking does in fact exhibit one traditional feature of the liberal reinterpretation of the principles of 1789—which, as early as Benjamin Constant and perhaps even Tocqueville, redefines in a limiting way the modalities of popular sovereignty. We shall thus see how and why Constant, while recognizing the principle of popular sovereignty as the basis of any legitimate political authority, attempted to justify the poll-tax suffrage and even, in the spring of 1815, to inscribe it in the Acte additionel aux constitutions de l'Empire which he drafted at Napoléon's request on the occasion of the latter's return from Elba; at the same time that the constitution retook the steps established since the revolutionary year X and made only the most highly taxed citizens members of the electoral colleges,[22] Constant's constitution—the "Benjamine"—shied away from mentioning, among the "rights of citizens" listed under Title VI, any right to "take part in the formation of the law";[23] and we know how in a general way Constant consistently maintained that, though all members of society have the right to freedom, it does not follow that they also all have the right to take an active part in political decisions:[24] in short, though the citizens remain "equal before the law," they are not equal regarding the right to name the representatives of the people and hence to participate in the "formation of the law." Need we recall, besides this, how Tocqueville, while making the democratic revolution a decisive and "irresistible" element in the progress of humanity, mentions the perils of a government in which the people rule (the tyranny of the majority, the exacerbation of the selfish passions, the disappearance of the individual "amid the common obscurity," and the like)? Whether in Constant or in Tocqueville, the liberal interpretation of the idea of democracy testifies as clearly as possible to an indisputably clear reluctance about what surely constitutes the major political event of contemporary history: the emergence of the masses and their exigencies onto the political scene. It is from the perspective of this diffidence that we need to read Toqueville's address given on 12 September 1848 concerning the question of the right to work:[25] he attacks the socialists' demand for the right to work as proceeding from their constant tendency to indulge "man's natural passions" and to give as the lone goal of the social system the acquisition by all of the possibility of "unlimited consumption"—a condemnation signifying a critical relation to democracy, or at least to some of its tendencies: as seen here, socialism merely serves to accentuate a bad side of democratic rule, the one by which the principle of popular sovereignty risks becoming an unreasoning despotism of the masses. There is a certain continuity between Toqueville's critique and contemporary "neoliberal" criticism of the idea of social justice, and in this sense the *neo*liberalism of Hayek and the Chicago school[26] does not display any true novelty: the intellectual history of liberalism seems in fact to have congealed at 1848, when the second big push—which, in a certain way, liberalism resists—forced the masses' demands to take their place on the political scene, and the liberal version of the reference to democratic values seems to have fixed itself definitively at this time, following a practice of reference to human rights (whose modalities we shall specify), but in any case on positions that always more or less consist of making a distinction between the principle of popular sovereignty and the satisfaction of the demands of the masses.

On the side of the socialist tradition, we note a just as congenital reservation toward the exigencies of the law. Owing essentially to the historicist designs that socialist thinking, notably under the influence of Marxism, always more or less trundles along with it, this thinking always seems to have a hard time giving a minimum of autonomy to legal norms, autonomy in relation as much to politics as, more generally, to the historical process of which political transformation is but one aspect; most often devalued is the juridical reference—for if the order of values is reduced to the (historical and hence variable) order of facts, the law seems to be opposed to fact only according to a fiction, even a mystification, which of course contributes to the perpetuation of the fact.[27] We know what Hannah Arendt thought were the consequences of this historicist devalorization of the law: when the truth of the legal is merely a reflection of the historical process in which it is located, the law thus relativized—not only positive laws, but also the notion of a natural right of man as such—loses its authority and it becomes legitimate, so to speak, to break it in the name of a possible anticipation of that movement of history of which the law is but the petrified expression of a simple element.[28] Certainly, we are not claiming that socialist thinking is always doomed to follow this path inherent in historicism to the end and hence to reproduce all its perverse effects: but it remains no less difficult to dispute the fact that the reference to law, and notably to the democratic values expressed by the declarations' proclamation of basic freedoms, is not very robust in the socialist tradition—and this for largely intellectual or, if you prefer, ideological reasons. We shall for the moment limit ourselves to the revealing example of Léon Blum, whom we so often regard as one of the fathers of genuinely democratic socialism; in his address of 27 December 1920 at the Congress of Tours, this opponent of the advocates of the adhesion to the communist Third International nevertheless readily affirmed his agreement with them on the question of the dictatorship of the proletariat, even going so far as to state: "I do not think, although Marx wrote it, that the dictatorship of the proletariat is bound to preserve a democratic form. The very essence of a dictatorship is the suppression of all constitutional prescriptions."[29] And it would be easy to show how Blum, though he agreed with the majority of his party in condemning the Soviet's perpetuation of a regime of tyranny, still recognized that, despite these repressive methods of government, the identity of goals pursued (the changeover from the system of private property) made solidarity possible between the socialists and the defenders of the Bolshevist system. Nicole Racine, who has stressed this political constant, has clearly indicated how historical reasons prevented the critical view of the Soviet experience and the total privation of rights defining it—a view that certainly prevailed in the Socialist party between the wars—from gaining victory over the thesis of continued solidarity with the USSR: signing a pact on 27 June 1934 between the Communist and Socialist parties for united action against fascism, the two parties made an effort to keep their commitment to mutual abstention from attack and criticism; after the signature of the Franco-Soviet pact (1935), the majority of the Socialist party unconditionally defended the USSR: the debate about Soviet violations of democratic values, which Blum continued to deplore,[30] receded to the background when the necessities of a unified tactics made themselves felt—necessities which soon became imperative when the question arose of the exercise of power.[31] It will be agreed that this analysis could easily be pursued with regard to the most immediately contemporary version of these united tactics: as Claude Lefort has suggested,[32] even though "the experience of totalitarianism teaches that the destruction of formal democracy has coincided with the destruction of democracy as such," this teaching has been largely "unthought by the Union of the Left" precisely to the extent that drawing lessons from this negation of individual and collective rights would mean making a radical break with the Marxist problematic of bypassing formal freedoms; this break, calling for an unsparing examination of the ideology of the French Communist party and its totalitarian calling, was in fact hardly compatible, at least publicly, with the imperatives of an electoral union. Even so, it needs to be stated that though the historical adoption of this political strategy was certainly added to some profoundly intellectual reasons for driving considerations of law into the background, these intellectual reasons were in themselves, if not sufficient, at least *necessary:* how would united action, and even tactics, with a party seen as the accomplice in a monstrous sacrifice of law,[33] have been even conceivable outside a horizon where the juridical reference was, *in any case,* devalued in favor of the consideration of the ultimate ends of history? It's still the case that this twofold intellectual and strategic heritage continues to weigh heavily on a socialist tradition in which the valorization of formal rights is always liable to yield to the evaluation of a balance of power.[34]

One may therefore legitimately ask whether each of the two great traditions whose confrontation defines the core of the political debate does not present, congenitally, the very inadequacy that excludes all "possible compromise" with its opposite number: the congenital blindness of the socialist tradition toward the strictly democratic impact of the most formal of rights, the congenital reluctance of the liberal tradition to take into account certain of the claims (notably in matters of social justice) that the affirmation of popular sovereignty seems to entail—everything indicates that, beginning with the common reference to democratic values, two *interpretations* were constructed from it, two mutually exclusive *readings* emerged from them to privilege, on the one hand, the values of social justice, on the other, the formal guarantees of freedom. Though this fact is obvious (and recalling it thus seems banal), the problem, we repeat, is no less real: the common reference to the democratic tradition and to the Declarations of the Rights of Man that, since the end of the eighteenth century, have proclaimed the rights constitutive of the human person must then mask a very deep and apparently irreducible cleavage; *in this sense,* the idea of democracy suffers from an indeterminacy or even a double meaning which explains why the consensus about the values of democracy poorly disguises some very real dissensions. Thus, it behooves us to get to the roots of this double meaning by trying to see how the history of the discourse of human rights could allow for this ambiguity to be introduced. From this point of view, the real indicator of such an ambiguity—and what should give us a greater appreciation of its nature—is surely found in the way in which the history of the declarations has gradually conflated, among human rights, two types of fundamentally different rights: permissions and entitlements.

4. Permissions and Entitlements: "Political Democracy" and "Social Democracy"

Analysis of the intellectual history of human rights reveals an initial problem in the very determination of human rights. Though the political impact of this problem is rarely noted, the historical facts about it are well known, at least, and it will suffice to give a brief mention of them.[35] It will be recalled how the very *content* of human rights has undergone an important evolutionary change since the nineteenth century, particularly since 1848, a pivotal date in the history of human rights. We know that in the minds of certain figures in the February revolution—and not the least of them—the plan was not to break with the principles of 1789, but to bring to the inspiration for the first revolution (the struggle for political rights) a supplement necessitated by the industrial revolution and the emergence of the problem of the workers' condition: the affirmation of social rights. In fact, issuing from the work of a largely conservative and far from socialist-minded Constituent Assembly, the Constitution of 1848 proved cautious and rather vague. In its preamble, the constitution certainly states that the tasks of the republic include that of "ensuring an increasingly equitable distribution of the responsibilities and benefits of society, to increase the ease of each," in short, "to bring all citizens to an ever higher degree of morality, enlightenment, and well-being." The state thus proclaims itself responsible if not for the happiness, then at least for the improved condition of all the citizens, toward whom it acknowledges *"duties."*[36] This recognition of the state's *social duties,* however, is not yet accompanied by a genuine

15

proclamation of the correlative *rights* of the citizens: even if the preamble concludes by entrusting the republic with the task of working "with a view to the accomplishment of all these duties and for the guarantee of all these rights," chapter 2 does not mention the formal rights (the "freedoms") coming from the Declaration of 1789 among the "rights of citizens guaranteed by the constitution"—thus excluding, notably, the right to work demanded by the socialists and whose principle Tocqueville, backed up by Adolphe Thiers, contested.[37] The establishment of the Constitution of 1848 remains, however, a capital date in the intellectual history of human rights because for the first time a debate occurred about a new category of right that some people thought should be added to those stated in the first declarations.

The first declarations primarily and almost exclusively emphasized the basic freedoms guaranteed to the citizens and opposable to the state, whose limits they thus defined. The rights proclaimed in 1789 were thus *permissions* specifying the individual's intellectual possibilities (freedoms of thought, expression, religion, and so on) or physical possibilities (freedoms of work, commerce, assembly, and so on). The political impact of the proclamation of these freedoms clearly came about through describing the function of the law: "The law has the right to prohibit only acts harmful to society," that is, acts that would prevent someone from the exercise of one of his rights," which becomes more explicit in article 9 of the Declaration of 1793: "The law must protect public and individual freedom against oppression by those who govern." Certainly, as has often been noted, the Constitution of 1791 mentioned the necessary organization of "public assistance" by the state "to raise abandoned children, to relieve the infirm poor, and to provide work for the able-bodied poor who could not find it"—in which there has sometimes been perceived, as though in embryo, the principle of another type of rights that define not the *powers of acting* and that are opposable to the state, but powers of obligating the state to a number of services, in other words, man's *entitlements* on society. Though the Constitution of 1791 inscribed the recognition of these obligations in the "fundamental provisions guaranteed by the constitution," it did not make them *human rights,* however, for their enumeration in the preamble merely echoed the Declaration of 1789, which mentioned nothing of the kind.

So although the Constitution of 1848 itself went little further in this regard than that of 1791, the debate around it was the starting point of a vast movement toward the later recognition, under the influences of Marxism and of social Catholicism, of social rights. A third era of human rights—after the proclamation of the permissions in 1789 and the 1848 debate about entitlements—began with the Soviet declaration of the "rights of exploited workers" (1918) and with the mention of "economic and social rights" in the constitution of the USSR under Stalin (1936): rights to work, rest, material security, education, and so forth. Within the framework of democracy, however, it was not until the preamble to the French Constitution of 1946 that one sees the "rights and freedoms of man and citizen consecrated by the Declaration of the Rights of 1789" reaffirmed and supplemented with the proclamation of social rights: "the right to employment," "the right to defend one's job through unionization," the right to strike, the right to "material security," and, in case of the inability to work, right to "adequate means of subsistence."[38] And the Universal Declaration of Human Rights adopted on 10 December 1948 by the United Nations General Assembly put the finishing touches, a century after the debates that had inaugurated it, to the movement toward the recognition, parallel to permissions (articles 3–21), of economic and social rights (articles 22–27: right to social security, work and its just remuneration, to unionize, to rest, to an adequate standard of living, and so forth).

In recalling these historical facts, it is important to lay emphasis on the political stakes and significance of this substantial development in the discourse of human rights. It is not enough to note—as has Michel Villey[39]—the growing proliferation of rights thus proclaimed: the evolution is not merely quantitative but one *of kind*. Briefly stated, the gradual emergence, next to permissions, of entitlements whose number and content are a priori indefinable and thus variable ad infinitum,[40] introduces important changes in the conception of the relations between *society* and *state*. The proclamation of permissions clearly involved a theory of the *limits* of the state, conceived as obligated to limit itself to guaranteeing citizens the maximum of possible actions compatible with the existence of a society. The consideration of entitlements, on the other hand, implies that the state is expected to have the capacity to provide *services,* with a resultant acceptance of an increase in its power to enable it to respond to requests deemed valid. Thus, it is clear that through the privileged reference to one or the other of these two types of rights, two conceptions of *law* and of *democracy* are at stake:

—On the one hand, a purely *negative* conception of the law, which is limited to forbidding any attempt (by the state or groups or individuals) to forbid the citizen from enjoying his freedoms within the limits of their compatibility with those of others: a law that forbids forbidding, and whose function has *political democracy* as a stake. According to the terms of the Declaration of 1793, it is only when the members of the society are "free men" (article 27) that "sovereignty resides in the people" in an effective way: for all citizens to participate equally in the formation of the law—a principle of popular sovereignty and hence political democracy—means that, as a member of the sovereign, each person can form and express his will with "complete freedom" (article 26), hence that the law protects the natural rights of man as such.

—With, on the other hand, the introduction of social rights, the state is expected through its laws to intervene in the social sphere, notably to ensure a better distribution of wealth and to correct inequalities: the henceforth *positive* function of the law is to take a part in fostering a *social democracy* now aiming at not only political equality ("the equal right to take part in the formation of the law"), but also the at-least-partial equalization of conditions of life. Consequently, while on the horizon of the defense of permissions is the idea of a *minimal state* limited to protecting its citizens' autonomy, the horizon of the defense of entitlements seems to be a *welfare state* that, through positive benefits and services, can contribute to the birth of that "material security" guaranteed to every person.

We then understand why the division between permissions and entitlements now inscribed in the rhetoric of human rights seems to disclose the ambiguity in the idea of democracy. The split between a liberal tradition marked by a reluctance to take account of the needs of the masses and a socialist tradition characterized by the devalorization of law in favor of the consideration of the ultimate ends of history is also apparent in the two possible emphases in human rights and could be expressed this way: liberals have tended to reject entitlements, and socialists to accord a merely relative importance (except in words) to permissions. Here again, this twofold assertion might seem dogmatical: the rest of this study attempts to ground it—but it is already clear that an ambiguity has been introduced into the history of discourse about human rights, with the risk of muddling up its meaning and thus considerably weakening the impact of the reference to these rights. This ambiguity creates the need to determine its generative principle and to bring out fully its political consequences. It is also necessary to ask if the reference to human rights is, as such, condemned to this ambiguity—in which case, decidedly, the comeback of the reference on the political scene might well soon fizzle out, if only for the sake of clarity in objectives—or if the lasting rescue of this discourse does not involve a preliminary *critique* of it: a critique aiming not to discredit it, but rather to determine or to distinguish the heterogeneous elements that have gradually amalgamated with it. Besides, it may very well be that this preliminary to a less unreflective and more fruitful reactivation is also one of the ways to follow to try and weaken this split between the two traditions that have introduced their debate into this discourse, thus making it politically serviceable for antagonistic causes and causing it to lose all genuine impact.

It may be all the more readily agreed that this is also the point of a critical rereading, in the sense just indicated, of the tradition of human rights (to question the debate between liberalism and socialism expressed therein) when we turn our attention to a second problem marking the intellectual history of human rights: even before the appearance of the problem of entitlements (hence their inscription among human rights), the political emergence of this discourse gave rise to the problem of the role of the state in the process of achieving rights—a problem that came to interfere (we shall see how) with the problem of the integration of entitlements to determine two very different and even antagonistic practices of reference to human rights.

5. The Actualization of Human Rights: History or the State?

In recalling the political emergence of the reference to human rights, it should be remembered that this origin had two sources. The French declarations, first that of 1789, were preceded by the American declarations of 1776: the first Declaration of the Rights of Man is thus found in the Constitution of the commonwealth of Virginia of 12 June 1776, and we find the same spirit in most of the constitutions drafted in the thirteen colonies which the Declaration of Independence of 4 July 1776 raised to the rank of states under the invocation of the rights of man.[41]

No point today in reviving a tired debate as to whether these American declarations did or did not have a preponderant influence on the drafters of the French texts:[42] the proclamations of 1776 incontestably have in common with that of 1789 the affirmation—inherited from the whole tradition of modern natural right—that men are "by nature free and independent," that they possess inalienable rights limiting the power of the state, and that the bases of political legitimacy are found, according to the contractualist schema, only in the *consent* of individuals on the need for a government charged with guaranteeing these rights. Despite some difference of inflections,[43] one notes an undoubted "parallelism"[44] involving surely more a commonality of intellectual sources than a direct influence. On the other hand—as Jürgen Habermas[45] clearly emphasized—the *representation of revolution* that played a role in the process of establishing human rights in both cases allows for a profound distinction between the American and the French documents. The declarations of 1776 are based on the conviction that the *natural* function of society tends to actualize the rights of man *spontaneously,* provided he is left to himself and the state keeps its interventions to a minimum: by emancipating America from English administration, the American Revolution thus aimed uniquely to form a social space whose autonomization in relation to political power should allow for a free production of the effects of the laws immanent in society. Thomas Paine particularly emphasized this theme in the second part of his 1792 *The Rights of Man:*[46] the natural laws of the circulation of commodities and social labor, of which the state's only function is to protect, are strictly equivalent to the human rights proclaimed by the philosophical tradition—with the result that, as individuals obey these laws because they find their interests in them, philosophy need not pose the problem of actualizing human rights. In other words, the American Revolution merely created the *conditions* for the historical self-unfolding of the laws of social reality—a reality naturally supposed to be good when the mainspring of progress is activated, that is, the enlightened self-interest of individuals: natural right is not made positive by some politically initiated voluntarist correction of some corrupted social order that should be made to conform to an ideal of virtue; the process by which this natural right "acquires the force of law" proceeds only from "common sense"—that of enlightened self-interest—that preexists any initiative by the state and that by itself produces its effects in *history.*[47]

By contrast, the spirit of the French declarations represents the revolution as a radical rectification of society by a virtuous will and this in the name of a moral ideal. Paradoxically, as Habermas showed very well, the Physiocrats, the chief inspirers of the text of 1789, echoed Rousseauean voluntarism in judging that, "contrary to the liberal conception of natural harmony," natural right can acquire positivity only through political power: even though we find in François Quesnay an anticipation of Adam Smith's theses about laissez-faire, the Physiocrats judged individuals too misled by opinion to see the self-evidence of the natural order, and they expected a despotism enlightened through philosophical knowledge of the nature of things to *organize* economic flows and the free competition of particular self-interests. Consequently, the Physiocrats and Rousseau are in agreement in not recognizing any "separation in principle of human rights from citizens' rights, of fundamental rights prior to the state from those conferred by the state"[48]—the actualization of human rights thus being thought of following a *political* model, as a process going, as it were, *from the top down,* starting with the enlightened initiative of the state: the contrast then becomes clear between the spirit of the American declarations, in which the actualization of rights refers to a *historical* process coming about *from the bottom up,* starting with the interplay of the enlightened self-interests of individuals.[49]

For the moment we shall not discuss this duality about which it is important merely to stress the political impact and consequences. In *On Revolution,* Hannah Arendt confined herself to seeing the difference between these two models as the contrast between a "political revolution" (the American one) and a "social revolution" (the French one)[50]—the former containing as its project a simple limitation of the power of the state, the latter aiming to create a completely new social order. The interpretation is surely not false—it's in this sense that there might be some interference in the subsequent history of human rights between the problem of actualization and the later problem of the *content* of these rights (freedoms, entitlements).[51] But we still have to perceive that the principle of this duality between the spirits of 1776 and 1789 resides primarily in two antithetical representations of history, as Habermas points to very well: "in the one place it is a matter of setting free the spontaneous forces of self-regulation in harmony with Natural Law, while in the other, it seeks to assert for the first time a total constitution in accordance with Natural Law against a depraved society and a human nature which has been corrupted."[52] In other words:

—The American conception, which assuredly has liberalism as a *political* horizon (the egoism of particular interests can be given free rein, with resultant progress in actualizing the content of the declarations), *philosophically* presupposes a conception of history in which the real (the social) is supposed to link up by itself with the

21

ideal (human rights) through the simple immanent interplay of social relations impelled by the seeming opposite of the law (the selfishness of private interest): such a vision of history is already highly reminiscent of the rationalist philosophies of historical development, whose model was to be fully elaborated by Hegel using the design of the "cunning of reason."[53]

—The French conception, whose *political* horizon is the (at least *Jacobin*) idea of an omnipotent and constantly active power,[54] *philosophically* assumes a voluntarist and ethical conception of progress—that is, a *practical* philosophy of history in which men transform the real from the outside in the name of a universal moral ideal (here, precisely, the content of the declarations, which *should* be actualized): such a view of history immediately calls to mind the ideas of *praxis,* beginning with the idea that the young Fichte was to develop of it in 1793, precisely to defend the French Revolution.[55]

At the political emergence of the reference to human rights, the problem of the modalities of their actualization (assigned either to *history* as a spontaneous process or to the *state* as the place of regenerative praxis) thus brings about a duality that is constantly encountered at the heart of the opposition between the liberal and the socialist traditions. Not, as we shall see, that too simple a correspondence should be made between the liberal tradition and the spirit of the American tradition, or between the socialist tradition and the spirit of the French Revolution: the transmission of heritages has proven far more complex—but it remains no less clear that a choice of one or the other of the two "revolutionary" models, in their aspects as conceptions for making rights into realities, was to be a constant element in the persistent split in our political universe.

The nature of the American and French responses to the problem of actualizing human rights has an additional interest. These responses not only prefigure some of the most characteristic aspects of the liberal and socialist conceptions of establishing democracy. Paradoxically, however, through their symmetrical and inverse drawbacks, the two conceptions also prefigure some of the most contemporary dimensions of the negation of democratic values—thus confirming, if need there be for it, that the democratic idea is more the pinpointing of a problem than the indication of a solution. This paradox can be explained quite simply:

—The French conception of the historical actualization of human rights rests, as we said, on a voluntaristic and ethical view of history: no one now doubts that the risk inherent in such a view is the historically verifiable one of the Terror:[56] if human rights do indeed represent a universal and unconditionally valorizable idea, how can we lose the conviction that any transformation (even violent) of the real that makes progress in actualizing this ideal is a victory for humanity? Since Hegel and his repeated criticism of Fichte's conception of the progress of law,[57] the relation between the "moral view of the world" and "terror" is sufficiently well known to make clear the danger of this first type of solution to the problem of actualizing the content of the declarations. The heritage of Jacobinism is no longer claimed, at least explicitly, as the possible nourishment for a defense of human rights.

—The American conception of the establishing of natural rights clearly avoids the risk of terrorism, since here it is clear that the social reality is not to be externally directed toward an ideal that this reality is supposed to link up with by itself, through the simple historical mechanism. The risks of this position are, however, just as evident. Not only is it somewhat precarious to ground human rights on the interplay of self-interest; from the perspective of this utilitarianism, aren't human rights too readily vulnerable to Marx's criticism in his *Jewish Question,* who makes of them the rights of the selfish member of bourgeois society? Above all and more seriously, however, to think of actualizing natural right as a movement immanent in history, to make of rights the necessary result of a historical process, is a structure of thought that takes the name of *historicism,* which (we now know all too well how) by granting no autonomy to the legal sphere in relation to the historical process, contributes to relativizing and eventually devaluing the juridical reference in favor of the consideration of the ends of history. As we go along, we once again encounter the conceptual figure of historicism, but through the persistent seductiveness it exercises on the socialist tradition, we have already sufficiently indicated its perverse effects to make plain that any appeal to this model runs substantial risks.

Enjoined, when confronting the problem of actualizing human rights, to choose between terrorism and historicism, juridical humanism thus seems fated to participate in one or the other of the two most radical modern moral negations of law and of democratic values whether it likes it or not. Through an odd paradox, the first Declarations of the Rights of Man—those of 1776 and 1789—already include the possibility of a negation of what they proclaim. How, under these circumstances, not to heed the most radical critiques of the discourse of human rights—whether they are found in a legal writer like Michel Villey or in thinkers who, like Hannah Arendt or Leo Strauss, have assembled their political thinking on Heidegger's deconstruction of modernity? Faced with this *internal* difficulty in juridical humanism, one might be highly tempted to subscribe to the overall thesis that motivates these callings into question: through the discourse of human rights, wouldn't modernity—from which this discourse is, as we shall see, strictly inseparable—once again represent the dialectics that, tragically, structures it and would condemn a defense of humanity as such to turn into its opposite and produce the worst negations of the human? As a new episode in the dialectics of the Enlightenment, should the fate of juridical humanism then teach us to dissociate criticism of totalitarianism from the reference to human rights?

So, when all is said and done, human rights need to be interrogated in three directions:

(1) If their proclamation does not constitute a politics, what *status* should the discourse of human rights be granted in relation to the political theories associated with them?

(2) What *content* are we to attribute to this discourse? Does the integration of entitlements with permissions attest to an insuperable political ambiguity in the reference to human rights, an ambiguity exploitable by both the liberal tradition in the name of freedom and the socialist tradition in the name of entitlements?.

(3) What *weight,* finally, should we accord the proclamation of the right of man, if we should become aware that—through the problem of the bringing into reality of the various declarations' contents—juridical humanism risks dragging along with it intellectual configurations (ethical voluntarism, historicism) containing the seeds of radical negations of rights?

The last question means that a return must be made to that modernity in which the reference to human rights appeared. It would involve an *ethnological* approach to our modernity to determine the place, meaning, and function that juridical humanism is to have in it: what is a cultural sphere like in which the discourse of human rights is a characteristic political element? To ask this question is to try first, vis-à-vis modernity, to adopt the distance necessary to the anthropologist's gaze: to determine the conditions of possibility for a juridical humanism, we thus need to start with ancient conceptions of law to show how the very notion of human rights would have been inconceivable in them, and then to see modernity in contrast emerge as the natural place for a new idea of law; only then will it be possible to define how, within modernity itself, the main difficulties come about, creating the risk that, were it not to overcome them, the discourse of human rights would condemn itself to perish.

Philosophy of
Human Rights

Ancient Natural Right
versus Human Rights

Because we are confronting the tragic destiny of a modernity that, though the scene of the proclamation of the rights of man, has also brought about their most frightful negations through the actions of totalitarian regimes, it has for some years become a ritual to blame modernity itself. More precisely, the relation between modernity and the idea of those rights it repeatedly and insistently proclaims seems to create a problem—to the point that for some of its defenders, a genuine reactivation of juridical humanism seems to call for a criticism of modernity. At first sight, the ritual displays a hardly unobjectionable prudence: if the modern emergence of human rights already contains the intellectual seeds of their most radical negation, shouldn't the defense of human rights aim first to free juridical humanism from whatever it is in modernity that risks perverting its values?

1. To Defend Human Rights against Modernity?

The recent return to juridical humanism is in fact most often accompanied by a warning against certain intellectual dimensions of this modernity that nevertheless produced the Declarations of the Rights of Man. We confine ourselves to a brief reminder of what has become almost a commonplace.

Clearly, the resuscitated practice of referring to rights as values that are irreducible to this or that element of the social process assumes a break with "many historical analyses" that "had demystified the claim to express some transcendence"—and so, for "the declarations that designate something *unsurpassable* to regain some authority," we would have to give up the message of "the philosophies of history and progress": in their claim to "explain the movement of universal history," these philosophies end up considering every human phenomenon—intellectual or institutional, for example—as a historical product, inscribing itself in a global process that, after bringing about this phenomenon according to knowable laws, will surpass it in conformity with the unyielding logic of these same laws.[1] In other words, it would be indispensable first to defend human rights against those rationalist philosophies of history that, clearly sharing in the modern project to subject all reality to the mastery of reason, intend to show how, according to Hegel's formula, "everything in history has unfolded rationally": if the logic of history is the key to everything that happens, the values of juridical humanism are strictly *relative* to the historical moment of their appearance; they are thus in no way "unsurpassable," for, as Engels serenely put it, "everything born deserves to perish"—in which we find the now-familiar idea that transgressing these values is basically just to get a jump, in the name of the direction of history, on the necessary process of their withering away. Such philosophies of history thus very clearly contain the principle of a negation of the values of juridical humanism.

We can make a more precise identification of what in modernity is indicted by way of an often vague accusation against "the" philosophy of history by naming it *historicism,* with the meaning Leo Strauss gave it in his *Natural Right and History,* that is, the thesis that "all human thought is historical and hence unable to grasp anything eternal" (*NRH,* 12). If we temporarily disregard Strauss's own position on the idea of right inscribed in the tradition of human rights, then, according to *Natural Right and History,* all of modern philosophy, since Machiavelli and Hobbes, leads to historicism: through Hegel's identification of the real and the rational, what was on the way since "Machiavellian realism" has been brought about, that is, a rationalist and dialectical philosophy of history has emerged in which the ideal (the rational, identified with the true and the good) is not opposed to the real, but is realized by itself within the real through the mediation of its apparent opposite; according to this theoretical structure, the same one as the "theory of the cunning of reason," the ideal cannot be opposed to the real to judge it: the distinction between the real and the ideal is actually just a moment which, being such, should produce its own "supersession" in the process of the self-unfolding of the ideal in the real—and this is the sense in which both Hegel and Marx can criticize any notion of an "abstract right" conceived as a transcending authority for the sake of which positivity could be judged and denounced.[2] The antijuridical impact of historicism is thus clear: far from the historical having to be judged by the criteria of rights and of the law, history itself, as we know, becomes the "tribunal of the world," and right itself must be thought of as based on its insertion in historicity.

We shall not elaborate here on Strauss's interpretation of the historicist calling of all modernity; nor shall we recall what we believe is its doubtful homogenization of the *variety of* modern philosophies of history.[3] What does deserve emphasis, on the other hand, is that, based on this (correct) designation of historicism as an intellectual obstacle to any affirmation of some transcendence of legal values,[4] the (simplistic) portrayal of the whole of modern philosophy as univocally historicist *should* evoke, in the new defenders of human rights, a sympathy for the most radical criticisms of modernity. We come back to this at the end of this chapter when we identify the problems with such antimodern defenses of human rights, but we can already understand why the revivals of the discourse of human rights are very often thought to find their philosophy of reference in the phenomenological tradition. For if, for reasons that are all too evident, one could scarcely mobilize Heidegger's philosophy at least directly (in this context it was hard to forget the wanderings of 1933), Heidegger's legacy to Maurice Merleau-Ponty or Hannah Arendt had to appear as what needed to be learned to be managed so as to preserve the reference to human rights from what in modernity threatened to take away all its meaning.[5] The problem is still that of determining to what degree this antimodern defense of human rights does not constitute a *contradictio in adjecto,* so to speak, and of whether, by situating itself inside this theoretical framework, the return to human rights has found the philosophy it deserves.

2. Going Back to the Ancients to Renew the Idea of Right? (Leo Strauss and Michel Villey)

Whether or not historicism, as a *theoretical* negation of right, is consubstantial with modernity, it is still a product of our philosophical rationality. Furthermore, on the *practical* level, it might be tempting to find in the rationalized organization of contemporary totalitarian systems the proof that the productions of modern reason, far from being contemporary, contribute to man's enslavement and to the destruction of his dignity. It could assuredly seem a legitimate move to renew the idea of right by seeking to escape this modernity which a mysterious dialectics, in the guise of "entering into a truly human condition," causes to "sink into a new kind of barbarism":[6] the goal of the Enlightenment was "to liberate men from fear and establishing their sovereignty"; today "the fully 'enlightened' earth radiates disaster triumphant";[7] thus couldn't this "program of the Enlightenment"—to make man sovereign—be more faithfully carried out against the Enlightenment itself, that is, through a process of trying to extricate itself from that modernity various themes of which were combined in the Enlightenment? The return to the classics, the gesture common to the various phenomenological criticisms of modernity, finds there its apparently least debatable support.[8] But we must resist the temptation of such a gesture, gauge its effects with a level head.

Whether we take as evidence the writings of Leo Strauss or those of Michel Villey,[9] the return to the ancient conception of law and right initially seems to offer a possible alternative to the modern dissolution of the juridical into the historical. In this regard, three characteristics can be identified as constitutive of classical, and particularly Aristotelian, thinking about right.

(1) The classical idea of law is defined by the discovery, against the authority of tradition, of the notion of nature understood as a "standard." On this point Strauss says: "Originally, the authority par excellence or the root of all authority was the ancestral. Through the discovery of nature, the claim of the ancestral is uprooted; philosophy appeals from the ancestral to the good, to that which is good intrinsically, to that which is good by nature.... By uprooting the authority of the ancestral, philosophy recognizes that nature is *the* authority" (*NRH,* 91–92). Thus, here the idea of a *natural right* emerges and, taking the place of ancestral right (i.e., in fact, the right sanctioned by history), enables thinking to transcend the real, to get beyond positivity, and to judge it on the basis of consideration of the best (the *just*) regime. Thus occurs the *autonomization* of right, as much in relation to history (as tradition) as to politics: as Michel Villey stresses,[10] Aristotle does not reduce legal work to the collection and application of positive laws inherited from the past or instituted by political authority (hence neither historicism nor juridical positivism), but the source of the law and that which can even intervene to correct the written laws and nuance their application is the consideration of the naturally just.[11]

(2) To give a better characterization of this classical conception of right, we need to state what notion of nature makes possible a distinction between the is and the ought, between the real and the

ideal—a distinction that gives meaning to the very idea of right. We first note that, by adopting "nature" as a criterion (standard) of the just, the ancients, unlike the moderns, take as a norm not the *subject*'s reason but a substantial element, the cosmic order that, because it is independent of the subject, constitutes a dimension of *objectivity*. Against the "subjective right" of the moderns, ancient natural right thus proposes the model of an "objective right" that is not deduced from the requirements of human reason, but can be observed and discovered in nature. Then, to grasp how the observation of nature makes it possible to determine what is "just," we should recall how the Greeks conceived of this nature: "Natural right in its classic form is connected with a teleological view of the universe" (*NRH*, 7). From Aristotle's *Physics*, we know what portrayal of the universe the Greeks formed[12]—to limit ourselves to the main points:

—A closed (circular) world in which, consequently, everything is locatable: while in the Newtonian universe the infinity of space rules out the possibility of something other than relative (to the observer) places, from the fact of this closure the Greek cosmos allows for the appearance of qualitatively different places that are thus not neutral or equivalent.

—A hierarchical world: in this universe with its absolute high and low, objects occupy a certain "station" in space according to their nature, the station that "is rightful" to them. Thus the heavy objects move downward not as the effect of some force of attraction, but because their natural place (the one suited to their nature) is located toward the low.

—A purposeful world: in virtue of this theory of natural stations, the fact that objects move is not explained by impact, the efficient cause of movement for the moderns,[13] but the cause of the movement is a *final* cause: objects move so as to regain their natural place, so as to occupy the place in the cosmos that corresponds to their nature and in which their essence is consequently realized. Thus nature itself is the principle of movement, which happens only insofar as an object has been driven from its natural place by some other object tending toward its own place: consequently the movement of the object ceases when it has regained its place.[14]

This brief evocation of Aristotle's cosmology suffices to explain the meaning of the designation of nature as the criterion of the just. Right can be determined by considering the order of the world in which everything that exists has, by virtue of its nature, something like a right to occupy its proper place and where it attains the perfection of its essence: thus the just, for a given thing, is what corresponds to its natural end (its *telos*)—injustice, at the level of human actions, appearing as analogous to what Aristotle called, from the global viewpoint of the *Physics,* a "violent movement" or, in other words, a movement by which some reality drives another one out of its natural place and prevents it, so to speak, from being what it is. If injustice in this precise sense is some violence done to nature, positive laws should express as adequately as possible this natural justice that is both *objective* (inscribed in the nature of things) and *transcendent* (insofar as nature thus conceived is an end, a destination toward which each thing should aim).

(3) A final characteristic directly follows from this ancient idea of right: if the natural law of the just, the objective basis of right, is determined as the rightful place for something in the purposeful cosmos, the science of right is defined not as the one that lays down rules of conduct, but as the science of distribution or division—in the sense of the formula of Roman law: *suum cuique tribuere* (to give to each what is his due); in other words, here justice is primarily conceived as distributive justice.[15] It may be added that, because justice is inscribed in the very nature of things, the method of the law will essentially involve the observation of nature and reasonable discussion to determine what is rightful for each person according to the natural hierarchy of the cosmos: through this reasonable discourse growing not out of premises posited a priori, but from the observation of the real, we recognize what for Aristotle defines dialectics and, in the perspective of a return to the ancients, ought thus to appear the true logic of right.[16]

Once the main features of the classical conception of right have been schematized, we easily see why the return to the ancients, assuming that is imaginable, could be deemed the decisive step in the attempt to renew the idea of right going against its modern dissolutions. The seeming fruitfulness of the return to ancient natural right can even be designated in a twofold respect—meaning with regard to the two theoretical configurations that Strauss saw as contributing the most, among the moderns, to nullify the political impact of the reference to right:

—As we said, the return to the ancients seems at first to have an undeniable *antihistoricist* impact: when we admit that historicism, particularly in its rationalist version (culminating in Hegeliano-Marxism), denies any discrepancy between the ideal and the real, but

reduces the order of *values* to that of *facts* (the just is what is historically sanctioned or ratified),[17] an idea of right that found its source in
classical conceptions would recapture a sense of transcendence—
since the norm is found in the best possible actualization of nature
as *trend:* thus, the just is not what *is,* but what *ought to be.* As Aristotle
clearly indicated in his *Nicomachean Ethics* (V, 10, 1135 a 3–5), the
reference to natural right then recovers the political (critical) function, which, though the form of government may vary according to
time and place, "there is still only one single form of government
that is always the best according to nature" and by reference to which
a divergent organization in a given city could be opposed.[18]

But the return to the ancients should also help avoid a second
theoretical configuration that contributes to modern negations of
right and that, to hear Strauss, paradoxically shows up even in con-
texts where the distinction between fact and values intervenes in a
principled way. *Natural Right and History* attempts to show how Max
Weber, beginning with a sharp distinction (of neo-Kantian inspiration) between the sphere of facts and that of values, also comes to
conclusions that are destructive of juridical normativity: as we know,
Weber rules out the possibility of achieving certainty or even a likely
opinion about an ethical or political topic and consequently maintains that the different systems of values, rationally equivalent or undecidable, correspond to choices that are completely arbitrary. If, de
facto, only the sphere of fact, becuse it is answerable to the principle
of causality, can provide the leverage for an effort at rational demonstration, the values elude explicative analysis and we must think of
them as stemming from arbitrary choices that cannot be *explained*
but merely *understood* by relating them to a project, to a choice that
is not explicable in terms of causality and whose validity eludes any
attempt at demonstration: it is evident that if the choice of values
could be subject to rational explanation, the choice would be classed
with the order of *facts* and would thus belong to the sphere of *nature*
or *being,* and not that of *freedom* or the *ought.*

To save the (intrinsically antihistoricist) distinction between facts
and values, Weber is led to the *positivist* thesis that values proceed
from "arbitrary" choices *strictu sensu* (proceeding from an arbiter
or, in other words, a free decision): consequently, value is created by
the arbitrary choice, and what constitutes value as such is the positing or instituting of the value through the subject's freedom. This
positivism—in the twofold sense in which only questions of *fact* can
admit of answers with a legitimate claim to universality, and that it is

the positing of values that gives them their validity—thus leads to the same conclusions as the historicism from which Weber meant to distance himself (*NRH,* 38): "Natural right is then rejected today not only because all human thought is held to be historical but likewise because it is thought that there is a variety of unchangeable principles of right or of goodness which conflict with one another, and none of which can be proved to be superior to the others" (*NRH,* 36)—in other words, because it is judged that there is no "true value system" but simply "a variety of values which are of the same rank, whose demands conflict with one another" in a conflict whose "solution has to be left to the free, nonrational decision of each individual" (*NRH,* 41–42). In short, here we find a relativism of values, even a "nihilism" in which it is scarcely possible to oppose to anything whatever that is a condemnation without appeal, for "every preference, however evil, base, or insane, has to be judged before the tribunal of reason to be as legitimate as any other preference" (*NRH,* 42). However we judge Strauss's criticisms of Weber's positivism, it must be recognized that (1) in making the case against historicism, it has the virtue of stressing that it is surely not enough to distinguish between facts and values to present before the tribunal of reason what is thus taken from the tribunal of history: the distinction between the ideal and the real is a necessary condition for any reactivation of the legal reference, but it cannot be the only one; we are also obliged to grant (2) that this underscoring of the trap of positivism may seem a supplementary argument for the return to the classical conception of natural right: for if the Weberian separation of facts and values leads to a (relativistic) negation of right, isn't it to the exact extent that the recognized transcendence of values is identified as the transcendence of *subjectivity* over the observable givenness of facts? If, on the other hand, we interpret the discrepancy between the real and the ideal, between positivity and natural right, not in the *modern* sense of the opposition between objectivity and the various subjective portrayals of the ideal, but in the *classical* sense of the distinction between the given state of a thing and what it should be and toward which by nature it tends, the (ethical or legal) ought is then inscribed in nature itself, in objectivity, and is, so to speak, readable in being—thus it is inconceivable that different and even contradictory versions of the ideal could be equivalent: the tribunal of reason regains its authority, it being of course understood that reason here is capable of observing an order inscribed in nature itself and not, as in the moderns, a reason presumptuously attempting to master nature and putting a price on things.

In summary, the return to the ancient conception of natural right has the double advantage of restoring, unlike historicism, a transcendence of the "just" (a distinction between the real and the ideal) and of anchoring, against positivism, the validity of legal values in objectivity itself—thus granting norms a strength that the anchoring of values in subjectivity threatens to take away from them with the moderns. Let us agree that the argument here has considerable force, and that it isn't surprising, in these circumstances, to find an evident sympathy for theses like those of Strauss there where someone sets out to give back to the claims of legality all of their political importance.[19] The whole problem, however, is that of whether all the implications of such a return to ancient natural right are acceptable— and especially the impossibility, obvious in any perspective of a return to the ancients, of creating there any philosophy of human rights. Do we have to grant that, to renew the idea of laws and rights, human rights have to be sacrificed?

3. Defending Human Rights against the Right of the Ancients

There is no doubt that juridical humanism is strictly incompatible with the classical conception of right, for at least two reasons that become apparent when we return to the Aristotelian cosmology that, as we have seen, supplies the framework for all legal thinking.

(1) This cosmology leads to a *naturalistic vision of politics* in which "the best regime" is determined by considering not human exigencies but the natural order. For both Plato and Aristotle, the art of politics, like any other art, consists in imitating nature, that is, producing an order in the city analogous to that of the cosmos—the criterion of the just thus being found more in *naturality* than in the humanity of any particular arrangement. Furthermore, Strauss strongly emphasizes this naturalism in his discussion of the classical modalities of determining "the good": because "all natural beings have a natural end, a natural destiny," the definition of this natural destiny (a definition proceeding from the observation of nature as the cosmos) "determines what kind of operation is good for them"— such that "we must distinguish between those human desires and inclinations which are in accordance with human nature and there-

fore good for man, and those which are destructive of his nature or his humanity and therefore bad" (*NRH*, 7, 95). A subtle and precise analysis that leaves no room for a possible inscription of the thematics of human rights within the ancient conception of right: quite the contrary, in Strauss's evocation, the classical determination of what is just for man appears to consider not humanity as such, but merely humanity as a particular element in a hierarchical nature assigning it a place and function; in this sense, it is the natural (of which the human is one dimension) and not the human that grounds the just: "'Natural' is here understood in contradistinction to what is merely human, all too human,"[20] in contrast to what is merely an artificial human invention, be it in accordance with the idea that man could have of his rights and, simple convention, is not inscribed in the nature of things. This naturalism thus rules out any basing of right on the idea of some contract through which free wills would agree on a convention defining the structure of the body politic: the contractualist model, cardinal in the moderns for whom it represents the concord of wills declaring the rights they mutually recognize, is by definition (at least in its individualistic version) alien to the classical conception of right.

(2) On the other hand, the portrayal of the world that grounds ancient natural right implies an inegalitarian vision of right; because the just is what is exclusively rightful to something by virtue of its nature and because natures are organized into a hierarchy, it is consonant with natural right that, by analogy with the theory of natural stations, those with a low nature are subject to authority, and that those with an elevated nature wield power. Thus here the principle of the just is not equality, but proportionality, that is, the establishment of a hierarchical order that imitates the cosmic order. This inegalitarian vision of the right is illustrated by the Platonic division of the city into three classes according to the natures of the individuals making it up—such that "each [does] his own work in the state . . . [such] would be justice and would render the city just."[21] Just as we know that in the *Politics* (I, chaps. 3–7), Aristotle declares the existence of masters and slaves "natural"—a division he judges "good" for both groups, for it is "natural" that the less intelligent are overseen by the wiser. It is clear that this conception of natural right, by definition rejecting the idea of an egalitarian right (*NRH*, 134), is radically at variance with the modern theme of "human rights" which assumes the affirmation of a *common* human nature.

Here we must commend the logicalness inspiring the work of Michel Villey when, convinced that only a return to the objective transcendence of ancient natural right would make it possible to escape the modern negations of the autonomy of right, he explicitly criticizes the discourse of human rights;[22] pitting the ancients against the moderns is taking account of the "nonexistence of human rights in antiquity," and admitting that "inequality is the rule,"[23] meaning de jure inequality. "The creditor cannot have the same rights as the debtor, nor the criminal those of the innocent":[24] perhaps *in this form* we will still accept, if necessary, the thesis the "*man* does not have rights" and "only *men* have *various* rights"—but will it be the same if, among the differences "according to which those proportions are calculated to be rights," we incorporate those related to sex, age, class, wealth, the role played in the social group?[25] It must be granted that, recognizing the value of the human person as such, modern humanism feels more than simple reluctance in the face of these conclusions that are fully coherent as soon as the return to classical thinking is made the condition for renewing the idea of right. In this regard it is significant to see, in a recent article otherwise expressing sympathy for Aristotle's juridical naturalism, Pierre Aubenque conclude his analysis by criticizing the texts discussed for never asking "whether inequality among men, as natural as it is, is compatible with the values that man carries within himself," and by agreeing that "whatever could be said against them, *modern* theories of natural right, of 'human rights'—even if this man is merely atemporal and abstract—represent some progress in relation to Aristotle's 'jusnaturalism.'"[26]

Having said this, it is clear that the antihumanistic consequences of a return to ancient natural right are hard to accept because of values that (modern) man carries in himself, but that by itself is not sufficient to discredit the gesture of a return to the ancients; if modernity leads essentially to the negation of right, it is absurd to protest against the ancients in the name of the values of this same modernity. There would be some injustice here in not reconstructing the whole of Villey's arguments against juridical humanism, and in retaining only his assuredly startling criticisms of the discourse of human rights; more precisely, to reject these criticisms in the name of the values of humanism would mean failing to see what Villey takes to be the relation between these values and the modern negation of right, and thus to contribute to the perpetuation of these negations.

A thoughtful defense of human rights against the right of the ancients thus cannot avoid a debate with an argument as sustained as it is provocative.

To understand the logic of the argumentation, we must recall what Villey (on this point again, very close to Strauss's claims) sees as constituting the founding or fundamental mechanism of the modern destruction of right—the emergence of an idea of right establishing *subjectivity* as the principle of legal evaluation, or, if you will, the idea of *subjective right*.[27] Unlike the classical thinkers, the moderns conceive of the right, as we have already noted, as deducible from the nature or essence of the human subject and not as an objective right inscribed in the nature of things.[28] According to this conception of the just, the right means the individual's "power" or "freedom" to perform this or that action—with, at the highest level, the subjective powers or rights of the sovereign, and, as a brake on the absolutism of this sovereign power, the natural rights of the individual, also understood here as "powers" or "freedoms": recognizing man's natural rights to a free opinion, the expression of his thought, and so forth, amounts to recognizing a certain number of "powers" in him that he may claim against Power itself and without which he would not be human, that is, a subject in contrast to simple objects. Thus, subjective rights (the rights of man as such) express certain possibilities of acting that are inherent in the *individual subject*—the jurist who draws up the list of these rights, here putting himself at the service of the individual—as Strauss also stresses: "the rights [of man] express, and are meant to express, something that everyone actually desires anyway; they hallow everyone's self-interest as everyone sees it or can easily be brought to see it" (*NRH* 182–83).[29] Endorsing the power of the individual, whose advancement defines all modernity, subjective right in this sense makes a radical reversal in relation to the classical conceptions in which right appears as a limit imposed by the nature of things (the world order) on the power of the individual (the law against man's hubris). Consequently, according to Villey, because the moderns do not see nature as the standard of right, any individual demand can become a right: because rights are posited only by individual wills requiring what the wills consider the conditions of possibility for humanity, "declaring" a right merely requires the forming of a *consensus* or the agreement of the spirit of the times about the recognition of this or that power as constitutive of subjectivity. Thus, on the very horizon of the notion of subjective right, the right could be grounded in a de facto agreement[30]—a reduction of right to fact that, being constitutive of juridical positivism, would destroy the dimension of right. The conclusion would then be called for that any conception of right grounded in humanism (on the positing of man as author and goal of the law) and culminating in the notion of human rights ends up nullifying the distinction between the order of fact and that of values, and that to renew the idea of right would mean "attacking humanism"[31]—both philosophical humanism (particularly Kant, "the Copernican who would have everything gravitate around man") and the "juridical humanism" that has been dominant since the Renaissance. Hence a criticism of the discourse of human rights as "a product of the modern age" and as a false antidote to juridical positivism,[32] of which it will be agreed that it displays not only coherence, but, through its rejection of any demagoguery, real intellectual courage.[33]

Defending human rights against the return to the right of the ancients thus presupposes not only moral indignation toward the inegalitarianism of the classical conceptions, but the ability to produce a genuine response to the argument just reconstructed—in short, a philosophically sophisticated defense of humanism against the objections to it based on the naturalism of the ancients.

4. Defending a Modern and Critical Humanism

For the discourse of human rights to fulfill its critical function vis-à-vis positivity, that is, established power, we must conceive of these rights in relation to some *abstract essence of man,* and this indeterminate idea of man as man must be able to constitute a value superior to all determinations impressed on man by his historical period, social status, or national identity. The valorization of "man without determination" that defines modern humanism, "a seemingly pathetic idea" without which, however, "democracy would disappear" and that "the entire critique of Marxist inspiration but also the conservative critique" have hastened to denounce: "Thus Joseph de Maistre proclaimed: 'I have met Italians, Russians, Spaniards, Englishmen, Frenchmen, but I do not know man in general'; and Marx thought that there were only concrete individuals, historically and socially determined, shaped by their class condition."[34] In this sense, supposing somehow the idea of a nature or essence of man and installing this idea at the basis or source of supreme legal values, the return to human rights is accompanied by a *return to humanism,* about which the least that can be advanced is that it is highly paradoxical in our intellectual universe, and this for at least two reasons:

(1) As Marcel Gauchet has stressed, this "man" whose rights are now being recalled is a notion that has been called and proclaimed outdated for more than two decades.[35] Such a "return of man" would thus also impose in our time a genuine turning in on itself and on certain of its most characteristic mental habits.

(2) Furthermore, in the political spheres where this new discourse of human rights is now practiced, and even though the Marxist component would determine reflection less than previously, the dominant mode of thinking is still much inclined to historicize ideas; the denial of essences, the desire to historicize or "dialectize" everything seems to have great difficulty accepting a reference to a sort of "universal" or "atemporal"—in short, to a suprahistorical value that seems to call for the imposition of a brake on the systematic relativization of all ideas. Here again, juridical humanism defines its practice against the stream of already ancient fashions.

When we add to these problems—which are *historical,* as it were—the theoretical problem raised by the criticisms of Strauss or Villey, it will be agreed that this humanism inherent in the tradition of the declarations of human rights deserves to be questioned about its conditions of possibility (or, if you will, of *conceivability*) in the area of contemporary thought. One cannot be content to defend the idea of "man in general" against the trend toward historicization of ideas by showing that this trend in fact shares the historicist relativism that undermines the autonomy of right, and definitively eliminates the very dimension of right: by suggesting that juridical humanism as such has contributed to bringing right and fact together and thus have engendered historicism and juridical positivism, Villey's and Strauss's analyses deprive a response like this of its force. Unless, of course, juridical humanism can be defended against these denunciations of those possible perverse effects.

Faced with these objections to juridical humanism from the viewpoint of ancient naturalism, it behooves us first to question the lack of nuance they display concerning modern humanism. Reading these analyses, one gets the impression that any valorization of an indeterminate idea of man amounts to making subjectivity the absolute basis of legal values: positing humanity as the supreme value here appears inseparable from what Heidegger described as the modern face of metaphysics, that is, the installation of the human subject, the *ego cogito,* as "the first and only true *subjectum,*" "the center of reference of being as such," master of nature and measure of all things.[36] On the basis of such an assimilation of *humanism* and *the metaphysics of subjectivity,* it becomes quite easy to object to humanism (including its legal versions) in the name of the easily established relation between the advent of subjectivity and historicism: we know how Strauss, following Heidegger, believed it possible to establish that the imperialism of subjectivity leads modernity to deny any transcendent standard (any principle of evaluation whose source is not the human will) and thus to produce an increasingly radical historicism.[37] So much that for any approach indiscriminately linking the valorization of the human subject (of the human as subjectivity) and the "metaphysics of subjectivity," the "overcoming of metaphysics," or at least its deconstruction, amounts to making a break with modern humanism. In this we find a clear symptom not only, of course, in Heidegger, calling for thinking "against humanism" and for considering that "[humanism] does not pertain to man simply as such"[38]—but also, openly against the idea of human rights, in Hannah Arendt. It is highly significant that, in the second part of her *Origins of Totalitarianism,* Arendt, whose allegiance to Heidegger's deconstruction of metaphysics is elsewhere made explicit,[39] wonders about "the perplexities of human rights"[40] and stresses how, in the idea of these rights, "Man himself was their source as well as their ultimate goal": "in this context"—said to be the one in which man has learned to master the real—it is humanity itself that should define the just, meaning "what is good for humankind," according to a conception of right in which consequently "the absolute and transcendental measurements of religion or the law of nature have lost their authority" and in which it becomes, judges Arendt, "quite conceivable ... that one fine day a highly organized and mechanized humanity will conclude quite democratically—namely by majority decision—that for humanity as a whole it would be better to liquidate certain parts thereof."[41] Following a line of argument we have already encountered in Villey and Strauss, Arendt thus decries the dangers she sees as inherent in the conception of right underlying the declarations of human rights—but by making quite clear the conviction that consistently motivates this type of questioning of human rights: juridical humanism is supposed to be a simple manifestation among others (beginning with the reign of technology) of the establishment of human subjectivity as the basis and center of the world, by which modernity contrasts with the age in which Plato could write: "Not man, but a god, must be the measure of all things."[42] Consequently, since human rights share the same conception of the real as that of which totalitarian phenomena are the worldly actualization,[43] escaping this fate would mean thinking against the imperialism of subjectivity, hence against humanism and human rights—the reason Arendt finds that, all things considered, Edmund Burke could be of some help through his defense, against the abstraction of the declarations, of traditional rights that, in every people,"one transmits to one's children like life itself."[44] In other words, against the desire to make a break—a sign of subjectivity and its claims to be fundamental, which is expressed in the declarations—the wisdom of tradition (in ancient times, "to be a slave was after all to have a distinctive character, a place in society—more than the abstract nakedness of being human and nothing but human");[45] against human rights, "the rights of the Englishman."[46]

Even if we admit a certain reluctance to follow Arendt's reasoning through to its conclusion, we limit ourselves here to questioning the principle of her condemnation of human rights—to wit, the assimilation of all humanism to the imperialism of subjectivity. We tried to show earlier[47] how, within modernity, the metaphysical (imperialist) face of subjectivity has already, in Kant and Fichte, been the object of a critique that could help a firm conception of the subject to escape its metaphysico-historicist fate; thus in modernity there are philosophical projects which, on the basis of a radical criticism of metaphysics and its illusions (particularly the illusion of a subject positing itself as Absolute),[48] have managed not to rule out all possibility of a reference to "man as such" and thus to ground a discourse on human rights[49] that was not rooted in a naïve metaphysics of subjectivity. We do not have to come back here to the philosophical foundation of this *critical humanism*:[50] to recall that, in the criticist tradition, it developed at the heart of that modernity wrongly reduced by the criticisms of juridical humanism to the various stages of metaphysics, is already enough to introduce some doubt about the relevance of these criticisms.

We add, in favor of the return to a juridical humanism, that the alternative proposed by its critics—the naturalistic conception of right—is not exempt from difficulties concerning its ability to restore a genuine transcendence. Not only would the return to classical natural right require relinquishing the idea of human rights, but in addition it is not at all certain that, owing to its conception of nature, the Aristotelian *jus naturale* is not already on the way to a type of thinking whose structure leads to the historicist negation of the idea of right as a fully transcendent norm. For in this idea of natural right, it is fundamentally the very movement of nature that fulfills what is taken for the norm; left to itself, nature achieves its ends according to its own immanent development, and (natural) right is thus merely the tool nature uses to accomplish its own ends; through the pursuit of what he has a right to by nature, each person effectively (in action) becomes what he already is virtually (potentially), and thanks to a just social division of roles and goods, he regains his natural place, so to speak, from which he can be kept apart only by the *human, too human* intervention of some violence done to *nature*. Under these circumstances, not only can we say that, left to itself, nature "is to blame" and acquires a sacred value that makes it possible to justify anything whatever provided it is natural;[51] but it must be particularly stressed that the theoretical structure underlying this portrayal of right is singularly reminiscent, mutatis mutandis, of the very one that in Hegel's historicism entails the negation of right as the ought that is *opposable* to the is, to wit, the structure of the theory of the "cunning of reason": for aren't we dealing here with a theory of the "cunning of nature," as Villey explicitly notes?[52] In this case what is the final transcendence of the perfection of essence ("entelechy") over the potential being that naturally (and *necessarily*) tends toward its realization? What is the status of the *human* reference to natural right, a simple tool nature uses to, as it were, dupe man into accomplishing nature's purposes? Hegel's celebration of Aristotle as one of his greatest forerunners thus was not, in this area, altogether senseless: Aristotle's naturalism structurally paved the way for Hegel's historicism and runs into similar difficulties concerning a conception of right. Already in Aristotle there can be no true separation between the real and the ideal, the is and the ought, fact and norm, for it is the very movement of the real (the natural) that actualizes the norm. In other words, here the logic of the fact is the actualization of the norm, and the aim of natural right is merely one element in this attainment of the *end of nature* (to achieve the greatest possible perfection) in which men collaborate without realizing it (without knowing, if we may say, what history—or nature—they are thus creating). There thus is much more continuity than disparity between Aristotle's *jus naturale* and the idea of natural right with which Hegel's historicism can still be identified, and it is not clear how the attempts to furnish Greek thinking with a renewal of the idea of natural right could truly rescue the right from its historicist negation. In short, as we know, *"there is nothing to be learned from the Greeks"*: we must think of juridical normativity *within* modernity, while knowing that this modernity could still deny, sometimes in the very name of those values it had created, the idea of human rights that makes sense only within it.

At the end of this examination of the critiques of modernity in the name of the idea of right (even, for certain of these critiques, in the name of human rights), the conclusion is clear and completely unambiguous. Certainly it must be agreed that *any juridical humanism* (if you prefer, any management of the notion of human rights) does not help free one of the (historicist and positivist) negations of the idea of right: there is an element of truth common to the anti-modern analyses, that of a warning about the risk (inherent in a naïve conception of subjective right) of reducing law and rights to the object of a momentary consensus that merely reflects the spirit of the times—a reduction we can agree would be the source of that proliferation of putative "human rights" so well attacked by Villey.[53] Nevertheless, we would be laying ourselves open to serious intellectual disillusionments if we did not also recognize these two established points:

(1) Radical antihumanism only fictively restores the idea of right and this in a form that today can in no way nourish the return to right as the essential element of politics. The idea of right that emerges from these criticisms of modernity surely finds its clearest expression in Heidegger: contrasting the primordial sense of *dikē* in Anaximander with "our juridical and moral representations" of right and injustice, he comes to the conclusion that, conceived of starting with being and not with the subject, "right" (*dikē*) is "the ordering and enjoining Order" different beings in the "abode" that, for each person, amounts "to his peculiar essence"; as for injustice (*adikia*), it would be thought as "disjunction" or "Discord,"[54] in short, as the violent intervention of human excessiveness (*hubris*) that breaks "the accord of the connectedness." In this representation of right, merely a less sober formulation of what we hitherto called "objective right," we are obliged to note that one will have a hard time finding theoretical material to support our modern indictments of positivity in the name precisely, of the "ought" that the real cannot manage to incorporate within itself as the immanent and spontaneous connectedness of its multiple elements.

(2) Consequently, all critique of historicism does not lead to a theory of human rights; correlatively, all critique of totalitarianism as the horizon of modern historicism is not accompanied by a revalori-

zation of human rights. This obvious observation should neverthe-less be kept in mind, for it has become so widespread here to con-found two procedures, although the examples of Strauss and Arendt again show that they can be unconnected: there is a way of criticizing historicism (and, beyond, its totalitarian effects) which does not open to any return to the spirit of the declaration of human rights, but on the contrary makes it possible to find in Greek slavery a sense of right granting the individual a greater dignity than there where one proclaims the rights of man without determination. The urgency, even the pathos, of the struggle against totalitarianism has thus led to combining moves that are in certain respects antithetical. In restor-ing the style of each of these moves, one certainly risks putting some idols of our intellectual universe between hammer and anvil: this is the cost of clarifying the debate, whether it involves criticizing totali-tarianism or giving the juridical demand its true importance. Outside the (by definition modern) context of a representation of humanity as subjectivity, there is no real thinking about rights that can oppose the values of equality and freedom (the very ones totalitarianism de-nies) to totalitarian phenomena.

C H A P T E R T W O

Modernity and
Human Rights

It is striking that the history of modern political philosophy has taken two very different forms: the tradition of *jus naturale*—which goes back to Hugo Grotius's *De jure belli ac pacis* (1625) and to which nearly all the political thinkers of the seventeenth and eighteenth centuries subscribed—ended, almost abruptly, with German idealism, and gave way in the nineteenth century to thinking of a quite different order whose primary object was by the society-state pair. This break is so sharp it would be no exaggeration[1] to say that before Hegel, the seventeenth- and eighteenth-century political philosophies were all doctrines of natural right: after Hegel, however, not one of them took this form: liberals, anarchists, and socialists of the nineteenth century wrote little or nothing about the doctrine of right or the theory of the social contract in the sense these expressions have in the tradition of *jus naturale*.

Why did this break occur? What is its relation to the question of human rights? As we have explained, the very notion of human rights makes no sense in ancient thinking. For it to get some purely philosophical meaning requires that at least two conditions be combined:

(1) Man must first appear in the universe as the highest of all values so that the idea of right is attached to him and he becomes the unique subject of right. Whereas in ancient thinking all animal and vegetable nature is in some manner the subject of right, in modern thought it is always in reference to man that the rest of the world has the status of a juridical object. This emergence of *juridical subjectivity* (of "subjective rights"), which must surely be Christian in origin, nevertheless got its strictly *political* impact only in the school of *jus naturale*. As Michel Villey has shown, the break with Aristotelianism was truly consummated with Hobbes,[2] and there that right came to be definitively considered an attribute of the individual.[3] More generally, we can say that with the appearance of the modern problem-

atic of the social contract and the state of nature, the notion of *legitimacy* became inseparable from that of *subjectivity;* only then was legitimate authority held to be one that has been (or could be) made the object of a contract created by the subjects who are in some way subject to it. Subjectivity (voluntary allegiance) was henceforth clearly posited as the ideal origin of all legitimacy such that the connection is made between the idea of subjective rights (grounded through and for the subjects) and the conditions of their political foundation. We need to take into account Rousseau's thinking even more than that of Hobbes if we are to grasp this first condition of possibility for human rights: for, assuredly, the *Social Contract,* and especially the theory of the general will, brought an end to the political reflection around *jus naturale* by depicting the conditions under which only the people can be regarded as *sovereign,* as the true *subject* (author) of all political legitimacy.

(2) This first condition (the setting up of the people as the sovereign subject), through which the legal notion of subjective right is incorporated to a problematic that is not moral or religious, but *political,* is not enough to account for the diversity of kinds of human rights: the crucial opposition between permissions and entitlements presupposes a clear thematization of the problematic of the relations between state and society—permissions pointing to a liberal theory of the limits of the state, entitlements implying both an enlargement and an intervention of the state.

Before taking up the questions prompted by Villey's criticisms of "the ideology of human rights," we need to take a closer look at these two conditions (the subjectivization of right in modern natural right, the appearance of the problematic of the relations between state and society as the center of political theory) without which the idea of human rights would remain empty.

1. Modern Natural Right and the Subjectivization of Right: Rousseau's Doctrine of the General Will, the Basis of Juridical Humanism

Contrary to what is suggested by the naïve interpretations of some social scientists, we need to recall that the *jus naturale* hypotheses about the origin of society have no claim to historical truth, as the formula of the *Discourse on the Origin of Inequality* attests: "Let us begin by setting aside all the facts." The concepts of state of nature and the social contract defining that origin are not meant to describe some past or future reality, but serve primarily a critical function as regards the traditional conceptions of authority. What's more, it should be emphasized that, if the import of these concepts is properly revolutionary, that is because they are quite explicitly fictions designed to undermine the two great theories of political power in sway during the ancien régime. As Robert Derathé has shown,[4] the school of natural right established a real break with traditional theories of sovereignty that located the origin of political authority in God or paternal dominion.[5] The distinguishing feature of such theories is to ground the legitimacy of power in an authority that is taken to be transcendent compared to human subjectivity—nature in the case of paternal dominion, divinity in the case of the doctrine of divine right. By asserting the purely conventional character of legitimate power, the theoreticians of natural right introduce the idea that the true (i.e., just) basis of authority can be found only in the free will of the people. By stressing that "civil association is the most voluntary of all acts" (*SC,* 95) for without any natural or divine basis only conventions serve as the basis for "all justifiable authority among men" (*SC,* 9) Rousseau quite consciously located himself in the tradition of *jus naturale.* Without going into the considerable divergences between the writers of the school of *jus naturale,* beyond the common background of adherence to conventionalism, we can note that Rousseau's originality was to trace down to their ultimate consequences the implications of this break as regards the philosophical representation of the notion of the people.

The conventionalist thesis is now considered self-evident, and it will surely be admitted—if at least one claims to represent modernity—that no one can be legitimately constrained by some authority that had not first obtained his consent *in some way.* The intermediate steps can be as complex as one likes, the idea belongs to the common consciousness or, to use Kantian language, to the "metaphysics of morals" that seem undividedly to prevail in our modern democracies; it serves as a criterion for making a de jure distinction between the just and the unjust at both the individual and the political levels. As excellent writers from Tocqueville to Louis Dumont have said, the logic of modernity is one of individualism: if, even before any further reflection, the very idea of a political authority transcending the implicit and explicit will of the people seems to us an unjust idea, the reason is that we are thinking of politics starting with what constitutes the essence of individualism: freedom conceived of as the faculty of *self-determination.* Every obstacle to this self-determination,[6] and hence to freedom, is then inevitably perceived as morally *intolerable* because in its most intimate being, it destroys the individuality that was posited as the basis and the ultimate end of any social order.

To return to Rousseau, what in this representation constitutes a real problem is the shift from the individualistic to the collective or, if you will, from morality to politics. To ensure the internal coherence of the conventionalist thesis dear to the school of natural right, it is effectively necessary, for Rousseau, that there be "some sovereignty of the people as of the freedom of the individual,"[7] or, in other words, that the people be thought of in their entirety as an individual, an entity capable of free (voluntary) self-determination. Just as an individual deprived of freedom—a slave, for example—is not an individual, but tends to be identified as a thing "for in being deprived of life and liberty . . . his very being is degraded . . . and destroyed as much as it is possible for it to be,"[8] to renounce our liberty renounces our status as men" (*SC* 10), just as a people who ceased to be fully sovereign would directly lose "its quality of people," ceasing to be an "association" and becoming a mere "aggregate."[9]

Hence two characteristics—indispensable to the constitution of the people as subjectivity—of that sovereignty that is none other than "the exercise of the general will": it "can never alienate itself" (*SC* 23) or, for the same reason, divide itself. In asserting the inalienability and indivisibility of the sovereign, Rousseau simultaneously contradicts and perfects the tradition of *jus naturale:* through his criticism of the people's putative right to alienate its sovereignty in favor of the prince or some representatives, Rousseau opposes all the writers of this tradition who believe that freedom of decision is a good that is legitimately transferable to others provided the transfer is voluntary. For Rousseau, however, such a transfer is not just illegitimate but senseless: freedom and therefore sovereignty are not goods for man to dispose of as he likes: man is by nature a free being; by freely renouncing his freedom, he in fact renounces himself, and delegating his freedom of decision would thus be equivalent to suicide. This argumentation, which underlies the criticism of the right to slavery, can be extended from the individual to people as a whole: "If the people thus promise merely to obey, it dissolves itself by this act, it loses its status as a people: the instant a master exists, there is no longer a sovereign, and at that point the body politic is destroyed" (*SC,* bk. 2, chap. 1). We thereby see that in opposing the school of *jus naturale* (which has, among other effects, that of a radical criticism of the idea of political representation), Rousseau is merely completing what is embryonic in the conventionalism through which modern natural right broke with ancient thought; strictly speaking, the thesis that political authority is legitimate only if it rests on the free will of the people makes sense only if the people in their entirety are thought of on the model of free individuality. And if the people are *one* free being, it cannot repudiate its freedom (alienate its sovereignty) without repudiating its own being.

For the same reason, and in the same ambiguous relation to the tradition of *jus naturale* whose ultimate consequences he brings out, Rousseau also asserts, against not only Samuel von Pufendorf, but also Hobbes,[10] the indivisibility of sovereignty. Indeed, if "sovereignty [is but] the exercise of the general will" (*SC,* 23), it is absurd to claim to distinguish different powers in it. The will, a perfectly simple entity, is or is not one, and cannot without contradiction be conceived as an aggregate of "fragments of will."[11]

Thus, for the first time in the history of political philosophy, the theory of the general will fully realizes and achieves the definition of the *people* or the *political body* as free subjectivity. This theory of the general will has been masterfully discussed by Alexis Philonenko.[12] We can only refer the reader to his interpretation whose principles we shall merely recall before drawing the consequences of direct interest to our purpose.

The main problem in the interpretation of Rousseau's theory of the general will concerns his distinction between the general will and the will of all in a famous passage in the *Social Contract* (bk. 2, chap. 3). We quote the text in its entirety so that the reader can bring it to mind in all its oddity: "There is frequently a difference between the *will of all* and the *general will.* The latter regards only the common interest; the former regards private interests, and is indeed but the sum of private wills: but remove from these same wills the pluses and the minuses that cancel each other, and then the general will remains as the sum of the differences."

What is surprising and needs explaining in this definition of the general will is the expression "sum of the differences," an expression that Rousseau repeats and particularizes some lines further on, characterizing the general will as a "sum of small differences." It is thus clear that the general will is neither unanimity, for it abstracts from the "pluses and the minuses that destroy each other,"[13] nor a fortiori the majority, for the majority, who can be identified with the will of all described here, is a sum of *common points* among the particular wills, and not a "sum of differences." As such, the will of all can go wrong, aiming at unreasonable particular interests: the majority, as everyone knows, is not necessarily right. So what is the general will under these circumstances? As Philonenko shows with great skill, Rousseau had an excellent knowledge of the mathematics of his time and in particular the infinitesimal calculus invented by Leibniz. This infinitesimal calculus served as a model for thinking of the general will: each particular will, as it differs from every other will and expresses an absolutely individual viewpoint, can be considered an infinitely small quantity. More exactly, the difference between the different viewpoints of particular wills is infinitely small each time. The general will is a summation of these infinitely small differences—in mathematical terms, an integral—while the will of all is a simple sum (addition) of whole entities (particular wills as they are identical).

To make this interpretation more intelligible, we can compare Rousseau's sovereign—the people as it forms a general will that produces the law—to Leibniz's metaphorical description of the universe in his *Monadology*. The inventor of the infinitesimal calculus uses an image that, mutatis mutandis, can be applied to Rousseau's general will: "And as the same city seen from different sides seems quite different, and is as it were *perspectively* multiplied, it also happens," writes Leibniz, "that by the infinite multitude of simple substances [in this case, the "monads" that human beings are—L.F. and A.R.] there are as many different universes, which are nonetheless but the perspectives on a single one from the *points of view* of each Monad." [14] What is true of visual perception is also true of right: each person tends to see the universe from his own viewpoint, and each particular viewpoint, each particular will, if you like, differs infinitesimally (by a "little difference") from the immediate neighboring viewpoint. Nevertheless, it is evident that for reason or for God (who sees everything) the universe is *one,* and hence that the different particular viewpoints are in *accord* and *harmonize* according to a formula that thus can be designated mathematically as an *integral.* If we consider the legislative assembly (for Rousseau, the whole people) as like Leibniz's monadological universe, the problem of the formation of the general will is perfectly analogous to the problem created by the fact that the universe is *one* but seems infinitely multiple to the various particular viewpoints: these different viewpoints are *integrated* so that, each being taken into account, the resultant is *one* will that is *general.* Thus, each person occupies a necessarily particular and different place in the legislative assembly, if only infinitesimally different from his neighbor. This difference is in itself legitimate, but to make the people *one* people (as the law requires), the difference must be brought into accord with all the other differences: it is incumbent that each the law recognizes his place in the community. Each person differs from all others in that his place is absolutely particular (like the viewpoint of each monad on the city), but, provided he desires the right, each person identifies with all the others in that he asks only for the recognition of his share. If we consider the political body a "primitive quantity," that is, a quantity created by the "integration" of small or "auxiliary" differences (differences between different particular wills), we can say that we must bear "the civil totality as the unique primitive quantity—the sum of the little differences"—and consider "the will of the particular individual as the expression of a little difference in relation to the will of another individual, thus as auxiliary quantity, given that it is admitted that in their common aim at the general interest these wills are identical."[15] In short, the general will that proclaims rights (proclaims the law) does not consist in a sum of common opinions, in a sum of identities, but rather in a harmonious integration, an attuning of viewpoints that are by definition different but in the best of cases having the same aim (the bringing into accord). We thus understand that the general will can be described as based on both the whole social body and each particular individual: based on the whole, it is the resultant or integral of all the particular viewpoints; based on the individual, it is, according to Rousseau's formula, "a pure act of the intellect, reasoning, while passions are silent, on what man can demand of his fellow man, and on what his fellow man can demand of him."

From the perspective in which the right expressed by the general will must take into account the viewpoint of each person as the limit of the viewpoints of others,[16] in the sovereign—or, if you like, of the people as they form a vast legislative assembly—there can be no factions or political parties: for making possible the mathematical "summing up of trifling differences" clearly means the quantities taken into account are infinitesimal quantities. As soon as "cabals and partial associations are formed at the expense of the great association, the will of each such association, though *general* with regard to its members, is *private* with regard to the state" (*SC,* 26), so that the particular point of view is not integrated in the social totality expressed by the general will. Thus it is impossible to form the general will; it must be replaced by the will of all, that is, a simple calculation of the majority, since the parts so formed are "primitive quantities whose power is measured according to the elementary laws of addition and subtraction." [17]

Thus, at the conclusion of this analysis, the general will emerges as the essence of the people as a subject producing legal authority: it is "the living nexus of singular wills—the law of interest common to the series of citizens, a law that without being distinguished from the wills that it connects, is nonetheless something other than the simple sum of these wills." [18] The general will—without which the people cannot be considered a true people, a sovereign, but merely an aggregate—then exhibits all the features of subjectivity or, if you will, individuality:

The general will is *one,* that is, perfectly *simple* and hence indivisible. In addition, however, it presupposes and expresses both *reason* and *will:* for in determining the general will, each person must confine himself to expressing what is legitimate in his particular point of view without overstepping his rights, his place, which implies that one "*reasons* in the silence of the passions," and that one *resists* selfish urges. Surely it is "utopian" to hope for such a will and such rationality from each individual. On the one hand, however, we may believe the egoisms will cancel out or offset each other—the reason why we abstract "from the pluses and minuses that cancel each other"; on the other hand, Rousseau is merely describing what would be (or would have been) a people/subject, without prejudging, at least at first, the chances of its embodiment.

To conceptualize the embodiment of the general will—now that we understand what it is—we have to ask how it can be particularized in its *source* and in its *application:*[19] questions Rousseau takes up in the passages he wrote about the *legislator* (who is, if you will, a particularization, at the source of the general will) and to the government (which is its particularization downstream).

We do not propose here to analyze the insurmountable difficulties that Rousseau runs into on this path:[20] we merely recall that on one side (the side of the government), only direct democracy seems a priori capable of not betraying the general will if it is true that "the more numerous the magistrate, the more the will of the body approaches the general will"; but, as we know, such a form of government would suit only a race of gods, and it is doubtful whether this form of government has ever existed. On the other hand, it is the very gulf separating man from God that makes a legislator necessary, for "the general will is always right, but the judgment guiding it is not always enlightened." [21] It is to say—this is the problem to be resolved by the legislator—that the will can be *formally* general, each particular will being taken into account and "integrated" according to the process mentioned, without it being possible to rule out that this will is, if not bad,[22] at least poorly or not at all informed in its *content.* Unfortunately, the person entrusted with providing good content to the form of the general will is himself merely human, while it "would take gods to give laws to men." In short, the particularization of the general will, both in its source (the legislator) and in its application (the government), would presuppose the intervention of the divine, and human finitude appears ineluctably to lead the philosopher to give it the status of a certainly well-defined but empty concept.[23]

Rousseau's thought is thus scarcely inclined to utopia in the current sense of the term. It even describes, with philosophically lucid despair, the ultimate aporias to which the *jus naturale* project of a purely conventionalistic foundation of legitimacy leads. If the general will is not embodied or particularized, the reason is that the finite human world cannot eliminate two divisions: first, the division between the people and the government, in which the general will always risks being betrayed—and absolute democracy, which alone would eliminate this division, is impossible on earth. Second, the division between the people and themselves or, rather, what they would be if they were enlightened and, by doing without the problematic legislator, could by themselves find some content adequate to the laws of their general will.

The relations maintained by the general will, as a perfect transparence of the people to themselves, and the divisions that prevail in human reality thus prove susceptible to two readings: one can, with Rousseau, start with the general will as the absolute criterion and deplore the divisions that prevent its actualization. But these divisions can also be taken to be essential and primary, and the notion of the general will considered only later. Under these circumstances the general will ceases to be an empty concept, a simple function of unhappiness, and becomes a "regulative Idea," an ideal that is no doubt unrealizable but comprehensible as the ultimate horizon of history, and not as a starting point that is inevitably followed by decline. This is clearly the Kantian interpretation of Rousseau, an interpretation of which we cannot overemphasize how far it differs from both the letter and the spirit of the *Social Contract.*

It could be said that Rousseau's problematic remains one of *essence,* accompanied by a reflection on human finitude. The *Social*

Contract's chief contribution to the history of ideas lies in the elaboration of a definition, even *the* philosophically rigorous definition of the people as a free individuality, and once the definition is produced, everything happens as if the accounting for the requisites of its embodiment had to lead Rousseau to a meticulous acknowledgment of failure. The big mistake here, however, would be to conclude that the recognition of the two divisions mentioned implies the abandonment of any reference to the general will as Rousseau conceived of it. It is true that nineteenth-century political theory was not a theory of essence or right, but reflection about those real divisions (people/government, people/people) that the *Social Contract* only points out as the locus of failure. Yet, just when these divisions become the subject of theory, the idea of the general will again becomes the bearer of a political project. Nineteenth-century political theory was indissolubly "realist" and "idealist," a *knowledge* of the real division of the social and an *idea* of the ideal unity—the idea of the general thus regaining all the robustness it had paradoxically lost in the *Social Contract* through the fact of its failure. If natural right is exhausted, if it even becomes an object of criticism and foil for political theory, it is not in the sense that it is radically done for, but more like an *Aufhebung,* a transcendence that preserves.

Even though, as it breaks with antiquity, modern natural right has provided us with the philosophical basis for the general notion of human rights (free individuality as the basis and limit of authority), we still need to see how the emergence of the major divisions between society and state makes it possible to think, against a common background inherited from *jus naturale,* the opposition between the different types of human rights—permissions and entitlements.

2. The Emergence of the Contrast between Society and State in Modern Political Theory: Permissions and Entitlements

According to a noteworthy argument of M. Gauchet's in his preface to Benjamin Constant's *Ecrits politiques,*[24] during the French Revolution there appeared the idea that the civil society might have its own integrity, an existence independent of some establishment by some explicit will—of the people or the monarch. And the liberal criticism of Rousseau—as it appeared in Constant or perhaps even more in the theory of national representation elaborated by Abbé Emmanuel Sieyès—provided the most explicit theoretical thematization of a break with the tradition of *jus naturale* seen finally, particularly in its Rousseauean version, as still a captive of the voluntarist frameworks of the monarchy of the ancien régime.[25] The liberal idea of the autonomy of the social would permit, or at least accompany (we are ignoring the metaphysical problem of the efficacy of superstructures!), the advent of the modern separation of the society and the state—a separation about which we have already suggested in turn made possible the distinction between permissions (antistate, if you will) and entitlements (implying the intervention of the state).

This reading, to which we shall return, seems to us basically correct and illuminating. Emphasizing the opposition between liberalism and Rousseauism, it leaves open a question we need to consider here: if Rousseau's theory of the general will marks the ultimate break with the ancient philosophy of law, and if it is as such one of the founding representations of our modernity, what is left of Rousseauism after its liberal critique? Must the notion of the general will be thought "archaic" when the liberal distinction between society and state with its assumed antivoluntarism comes into play? This interpretation surely has the merit of corresponding to the ambiguous image of a Rousseau who to the partisans of the ancients (Edmund Burke, for example) appears modern, and to the moderns (liberals) appears ancient. It runs into a fatal difficulty, however: it would be strange indeed that the work that through its theory of sovereignty makes a complete break with the ancient world, has left no legacy in the thinking of those who more or less trace themselves back to the French Revolution and were even its defenders or architects! The importance of this question for our subject is clear, and we can state it schematically as follows: as we explained, the notion of human rights in general presupposes the elimination of traditional naturalistic or psychological doctrines of sovereignty, for the idea that man is the subject of right rigorously implies a conventionalistic and subjectivist conception of the origin and legitimacy of political power. But, the moment it's set up, the general notion of human rights divides into permissions and entitlements, a division that surely presupposes another division: that of the society and the state, which is fully thematized in political thought only with the liberal critique of Rousseau.[26] If this analysis is correct, permissions and entitlements must, as species of the same kind (human rights in general), be somehow rooted in Rousseauean soil. Hence our hypothesis that modern political theories, whether liberal, socialist, or anarchist, are fundamentally rooted in the Rousseauean conventionalism they inherited, even if,

in a way that remains to be made clear, they proclaim—which is particularly clear for liberalism—a critical distancing of themselves
from the *Social Contract*. If, in insofar as it thematizes the emergence
of the contract between society and state, the liberalism of a Constant
represents a break with the theory of *jus naturale*, this break is made
against the background of agreement with what in *jus naturale* in
turn marks a break with antiquity. To be more precise, if Rousseau's
general will does not appear in any of the political theories as a *so-
ciologically* adequate description of that which constitutes the reality
of modern societies, which surely has to do with the contrast between society and state, it is still true that the social and political
unity aimed for by the doctrine of the general will as the seat of
sovereignty continues to ground and to animate *all* modern political
thought, even when it assumes the form of an explicit criticism of the
theory of *jus naturale*. Faced with accounting for the real divisions
shaping society, the general will, far from being consigned to the
museum of archaisms, becomes the regulative idea of modern political philosophy. Philosophically thematized, the emergence of the
society-state contrast, as it leads to particularizing the notion of human rights and giving rise to the important conflict between freedoms and entitlements, thus includes two elements: a liberal element best expressed in Constant's criticism of Rousseau, and an
element we can call Kantian by which, as the division is taken into
account, the general will becomes an Idea of which it needs to be
indicated how the various approaches are constitutive of the plurality
of modern political theories.

3. From Rousseau to Constant: An Antivoluntarist Idea of Civil Society

To consider only the basis of the opposition in M. Gauchet's preface
between Constant and Rousseau, we find it seems to crystallize
around four great themes:

(1) Despite the appearance of freedom it introduces, the idea of
the general will, that is, of man's mastery of society, with its correlate,
the sovereignty of the people, in reality it creates the conditions of
possibility for a new kind of dictatorship that is infinitely more influ-
ential than that of the tyrannies known under the ancien régime: because the will of the people is the sole principle of legitimacy, its
diversion to their advantage by a person or an assembly is enough
for them to be invested with absolutely unlimited power.

(2) Coming after Rousseau, the men of 1793 committed a radical error about the nature of the upheaval of 1789: the society that arose then was individualistic, centered on the principle of the "freedom of the moderns." From the viewpoint of this dawning individualism, the *Social Contract* inspiring the Jacobins represented a real archaism, or more exactly a freakish mixture: starting from premises that are modern, individualistic, and egalitarian, it still retains the need for the preeminence of the whole (of the general) over the parts. Thus Rousseau is not a "true modern": from the monarchy of the ancien régime he keeps the voluntarist idea of the *casual power* of society, the requirement of a primacy for the whole, even though this primacy is not embodied in the person of the prince, but likened to the entity immanent in the social that is the general will.[27]

(3) We are thus led to what may be the ultimate basis of Constant's criticism: political power neither is nor should be a transcendent (prince) or immanent (general will) cause of the social, but is to be regarded as an effect of it.[28] Thus one should give up the voluntarist myth that society would dissolve when it ceased to be continually created by a causal power (whether monarchical or democratic). The reality of modern societies is quite different: they have their own strength and do not owe their existence to political power; quite the contrary, as we see in Constant's theory of the law,[29] political power owes its existence to them. Individuals do not enter into relations among themselves because of laws, on the contrary: laws are the expression of preexistent social relations.

(4) Hence we can in a non-Rousseauean way distinguish between the society and the state: "With the appearance of a social fact which is its own originating cause," writes Gauchet, "which is thus the very opposite of a derived power, a *separation* is suddenly created between the strictly civil sphere and the political authority emanating from it," such that thanks to the affirmation of the *intrinsic* consistency of the social, there is "a *dissociation* in principle between what affects bonds spontaneously woven between individuals . . . and what concerns the role and tasks specifically delegated to the public authority"[30]—a dissociation still blocked in Rousseau by the voluntarist illusion which was in fact inherited from the monarchy of the ancien régime, according to which no society can exist outside a "power-cause" or casual power that constitutes it as such.

Constant's analysis shows a great lucidity about the nature of modernity and its most salient feature, individualism—even though, as Gauchet shows, it does not explain the growth of the state that, contrary to his predictions, was in reality to mark the evolution of contemporary societies.[31] Accurate as it is as a criticism of a Mably or a Robespierre, this analysis still seems to us to miss the true significance of the *Social Contract* and consequently fails to understand its continual revival in modern political theory, including of course among the seemingly least Rousseauean liberal doctrines. The point deserves to be made with some precision, for it is a matter of seeing how Rousseauism, the high point of the break with antiquity, is the shared capital of all modernity even when it seems to (and really does) diverge from it in this or that important respect.

It will already have been noted that for the most part Constant's criticism falls short of its target. We give some indications of this:

—The analysis of the dangers of usurpation menacing the general will and able to bring forth a new and unchecked despotism, ascribed as it is with unprecedented legitimacy, is surely pertinent. But it is quite astonishing to see this analysis directed against Rousseau: it is enough to open the *Social Contract* and pay the slightest bit of attention to the difference between the general will and the will of all to see that it doesn't mean anything else on the political level: for Rousseau, the greatest threat hanging over the social body lies precisely in the confusion of the will of all, which is often merely the will of a simple faction, with the general will. Rehberg, little suspected of sympathies for Rousseau, realized this and criticized the French revolutionaries for making this confusion and, betraying Rousseau, for bringing on the Terror.[32]

—The accusation of voluntarism (repeated today without major modification, it seems to us, by a writer like F. A. von Hayek under the term "constructivism") seems more serious. Here again, though it is a telling criticism of the men of 1793, it misses its target when aimed at Rousseau himself. The point is not to save Rousseau at any cost, but only to realize that the *Social Contract* is neither a guide to concrete politics nor a sociological analysis of social and historical reality. Here the status of discourse receives all of its importance. Falling in the philosophical tradition of *jus naturale,* the *Social Contract* for the most part raises questions of legitimacy. Nowhere does Rousseau say, as Constant's criticism suggests, that the social can exist only as self-established, continually created, as it were, by the general will. He says something quite different and infinitely harder to criticize, namely, that the law is *legitimate* only if it expresses the general will, which for Rousseau presupposes that everyone be taken into account. This is not a thesis about the conditions of possibility for the

61

actual historical existence of any particular political body, but about a philosophical requirement that seems to us still to describe adequately what could be called the modern political conscience and, as such, in no way represents any archaism. It thus does not seem to us that this requirement could be voided, and it appears in the liberal doctrines of representation, even when they appear to be (and on certain points, actually are) poles apart from Rousseauism.

—Finally, it is unclear to us that Rousseau entirely disregards the distinction between the public and the private, that he wholly reduces the freedom of the moderns in favor of that of the ancients, or even that he requires a *total* alienation of individual rights in favor of "the state." Understood correctly, from an exact interpretation of the doctrine of the general will and the law, Rousseau's thinking, as expressed in the famous chapter on the "limits of the sovereign power," seems acceptable even to a liberal viewpoint: "It is granted that everything that an individual alienates by the social compact is only that part of his power, his property, and his liberty, the use of which is important to the community; but we must also grant that the Sovereign is the only judge of what is important to the community" (*SC,* 28). This is clearly valid only if the sovereign is indeed the general will (and not the will of all, as Rousseau fears) and, as such, it can never set itself up for any particular object. Thus, through the limits that it imposes on the law, the doctrine of the general will is also in a sense a theory of the limits of the state, for it is necessary "to distinguish properly between the respective rights of the citizens and the Sovereign, and between the duties which the former have to fulfill in their quality as subject, and the natural right which they ought to enjoy in their quality as men" (*SC* 27–28).

4. The Limits of the Liberal Criticism of Rousseau: Abbé Sieyès, Paradoxical Heir of the Doctrine of the General Will

Thus, Constant's criticism must be relativized. As a proof, we cite the fact that Rousseau's doctrine of the general will is present in the liberal theory of representation as elaborated by the Constituent Assembly of 1789, in particular by the abbé Sieyès, and written into the Constitution of 1791. The assertion appears paradoxical: we have stated how, with the idea that sovereignty is inalienable, the *Social Contract* ruled out all possibility of representing this sovereignty. No doubt, Rousseau had to make an exception in the face of the classic problem posed by "big countries"; but the representation that he reintroduced was, as we know, accompanied by an "imperative mandate" through which the representatives depended closely on those they represented.[33] We can say that the liberal doctrine of national representation seems at first to be the complete opposite of Rousseauism because it is designed to do without that mandate-representation in which it sees—another archaism of Rousseau in its eyes—a pure residue of the ancien régime. How, under these circumstances, could the doctrine of the general will show up again?

Let us first recall that in the ancien régime the deputy, tied by an imperative mandate, is considered not to have an autonomous will but is, strictly speaking, merely the representative or, one might say, the *ambassador* of the bailiwick or the particular social order that has elected him.[34] The conception of representation means, on the one hand, that the representation is connected to *particular* interests (which contrasts with the modern idea that the deputy represents the nation as a whole), and, on the other hand, that the act of representation is not considered an *individual* fact (the vote being carried out in principle by order and, in the assembly of each order, by bailiwick). Therefore, representation in the ancien régime cannot truly be considered to share in sovereignty, but is limited to a consultative role.

It is this conception of representation that Abbé Sieyès's doctrine of national sovereignty was intended to overcome. Very schematically, we could say that it is opposed to the idea of mandate on three points:

First, and this may be the main point, the representative must not be simply the representative of the particular group that elected him, but represents the nation as a whole, conceived of, in the words of Sieyès, not "as a collection of states," but as "a unique whole composed of integrating parts." Clearly underpinning this new vision of representation is the emerging of the idea of the nation, indissolubly connected as it is to that of individualism: the country or nation is not thought of as a hierarchy of different orders by nature, but as an abstract entity comprehending a multitude of equal individuals. Within the legislative assembly the vote will thus be made per capita and not by order, and according to the Constitution of 1791, the deputies elected *in* the *départements* will not, for all that, be considered elected *by* the *départements* (which become simple administrative districts): "The representatives named in the *départements* will not be representatives of a particular *département* but of the nation as a whole."

Representation thus ceases to be a mandate, and as the representative rises to the status of an individual endowed with freedom, he ceases to be the simple element of an order that surrounds him and acquires his own will: at least from a legal viewpoint, the modern deputy is not tied in his legislative will by any commitment. So too, representation ceases to be purely consultative. What's more, it becomes the locus of sovereignty par excellence, for it is in and through representation that there emerges the national will that did not exist *before* the legislative body, but only *after* and *through it.* Thus, to limit ourselves to these few brief bits of evidence, it seems that with the liberal doctrine of national representation, we are at the opposite pole not only of representation in the ancien régime, but also of the *Social Contract,* for sovereignty is taken away from the people and goes over wholly to an assembly of representatives, unbound to any imperative mandate, and what's more, elected by suffrage based on a poll tax![35]

Nevertheless, when we take a closer look at the reasons why the theorists of national representation reject the imperative proxy, we see that they echo Rousseau's theory of the general will on more than one point: truth to tell, these reasons even retain that doctrine wholly intact apart from the fact that it is valid not for the people as a whole but only for the legislative assembly. Obviously, the difference must not be minimized. When, however, we admit the necessity of representatives (and Rousseau himself, as we have said, recognizes this necessity for large countries), we may admit that the doctrine of national representation corresponds better to Rousseau's conception of the general will than does the doctrine of the imperative mandate.

This is what clearly transpired in the important debate on 7 September 1789 between Sieyès and defenders of the imperative mandate like Pétion de Villeneuve.[36] Villeneuve's attitude toward representation is seemingly faithful to the letter of Rousseau's writings: asserting that "the highest degree of political perfection" would lie in the direct participation of individuals in forming the general will, he accepts the need for representation only grudgingly, as a fall from the ideal,[37] and corrects this fall by subjecting the representative to the claims of the imperative mandate.

Sieyès's response is striking because it, too, is made in the name of a Rousseauean logic: if by hypothesis the necessity of representatives is admitted (and Sieyès is clearly convinced that direct democracy is impossible; but wasn't Rousseau as well?), it is easy to see that by subjecting representatives to the imperative mandate makes it impossible ever to isolate something like a general will. Binding representation to the mandate is to admit that the representatives defend the interests of particular groups, but also express wills that (according to Rousseau's arguments in chapter 3 of book 2 of the *Social Contract*) are general only in relation to their group and particular in relation to the whole of society or, to use Sieyès's language, the nation. We have seen how the central thesis of the *Social Contract* was that the general will could be formed only if it issued from the absolutely particular wills ("infinitesimal quantities") of individuals who are also absolutely monadic, and that if "cabals" and "factions" formed in the legislative assembly, that was the end of the general will. Bound by a mandate, representation could not be regarded as an infinitesimal quantity, nor the representative as a free and autonomous individual. To defenders of the imperative proxy, Sieyès states that they themselves cannot "want a deputy of all the citizens of the kingdom to listen to the wishes only of the residents of a bailiwick or a municipality as the will of the whole nation"—which implies giving up the imperative mandate. As Carré de Malberg wrote very well, rightly pointing to Sieyès's paradoxically Rousseauean inspiration: "The general will forming the expression of sovereignty cannot be understood as a sum of particular wills coming from each of the bailiwicks; but this general will itself shares in the unity and indivisibility of the nation."[38] Did Rousseau ever say anything else? The introduction of representation into the framework of the *Social Contract* thus does not necessarily lead to giving up the theory of the general will: the general will is rather shifted from the people to the legislative assembly which is then distinct from it—the reason why, still consistent with Rousseau's logic, this assembly is the real locus of sovereignty, while the election of representatives is relegated to the status of a simple *function*.

Thus we see how the notion of general will can be said to live on outside the frameworks of the *Social Contract*, in this case in a theoretical space, liberalism, that might seem a priori utterly hostile to it. Certainly, it does not issue from the people as a whole, but from their representatives. A double division, inscribed in a veiled way in the *Social Contract*'s failure to particularize the general will on the side of its source (the legislator) as in its application (the government), is now clearly taken into account: the people are divided, if not de jure, at least de facto (into active and passive citizens, then into representatives and the represented);[39] and through its own autonomy, society itself is differentiated from the state, as the private is from the public.

Yet as a result, and this is surely the great difference from the *Social Contract,* the general will, whose logical (or mathematical) structure remains the same, becomes an Idea in the Kantian sense, by the very fact of the taking of these division into account. If, as we have suggested, the thematization of these divisions is the result of modern political theories, these theories can be said both to transcend and to preserve the Rousseauean legacy of *jus naturale.* So, to conclude this chapter we still need to look at how, in view of the recognition of the major division between society and state—with its consequent transformation of the general will into an Idea—the fundamental principles of modern political theories come to be. To our minds the shift from natural right to political theory is made in the framework of Kant's philosophy.

5. From Rousseau to Kant: The Systematic Foundation of Modern Political Theories (Anarchism, Socialism, Liberalism)

The originality of Kant's *Doctrine of Right* has rarely been noted. Following a long tradition, Hannah Arendt herself saw it as an arid, formalistic, and rather unoriginal piece of writing.[40] Because of its formally systematic (and not formalistic) character, however, this work is of exceptional interest: on the one hand, it establishes a link between natural right and what without too great risk can be considered the most accomplished expression of modern anti-Aristotelian moral philosophy, to wit, the *Critique of Practical Reason;* on the other hand, in establishing, beginning with this very link, a clear division between state and society,[41] it makes possible a glimpse of the reasons why, in the framework of modern political thought, it is doubtless possible to conceive of just three fundamental political theories: anarchism, socialism, and liberalism. The argumentation deserves serious consideration and clear discussion: for if it proves pertinent, it should lead us to consider that, against the background of *jus naturale,* and once the division between society and the state is set up, three discourses can be held about human rights in modernity: liberal, anarchist, and socialist discourse.

By positing that the ends of moral activity are not inscribed in a transcendent natural *cosmos,* but rather imposed on man by his own reason, the *Critique of Practical Reason* marks a definite break with ancient morality, comparable to the one introduced on the political level by the theory of *jus naturale.*

To be persuaded of this, it is enough to study Kant's remarkable doctrine of *imperatives*. Kant distinguishes three kinds of imperatives that can prescribe the ends of action in general:

(1) The imperatives of suitability concern the mean-ends relation and involve what we would now call "instrumental reason" or, in Weberian terms, "rationality in relation to an end." They tell us: *if* you wish to obtain end *X*—it doesn't matter what it is: it can be, to use Kant's example, either to heal or to poison[42]—*then* it is necessary to use means *Y.* These imperatives are thus about purely subjective ends that depend exclusively on the free arbitrary choice of each individual.

(2) The imperatives of prudence represent a higher stage and are closer to what Kant calls morality, though without yet reaching it: still instrumental and hypothetical, they involve ends that are *common* to humanity and not merely particular to each subject. The typical example is the pursuit of health which can be assumed to be a good for every individual. Here we are no longer concerned with pure arbitrariness and particularity; yet what distinguishes prudence from genuine morality is that the ends it helps to attain are common to humanity only in so far as it seems as an animal or biological species. It is at this level that Kant locates ancient morality, and particularly that of Aristotle, who makes happiness the ultimate end of ethics, whereas, through the quest for happiness, man is not yet distinguished from animality.

(3) The imperative of morality thus prescribes ends that can be chosen only by a free being: the ends of reason are not only common to humanity as a biological species, but also as the whole set of beings endowed with freedom and reason (not to lie, not to treat others purely as means, and so forth).

In going from suitability to prudence and then morality, one thus goes from particular ends to general ends and then to universal ends. The moral question par excellence is thus the following: under what circumstances can I think the ends I propose are not only my subjective ends, but also ends that are objectively valid, meaning admissible by everyone? Morality thus presupposes that one goes beyond his own point of view, beyond his egoism and selfish interests to consider the common good; this effort in turn presupposes freedom understood as the faculty of not being completely determined by one's selfish inclinations.

If we think about it with due care, we will easily see that these lucidly formulated requirements of Kant's clearly best express what could be called the modern consciousness of morality. Just as we always think of legitimacy more or less in terms of convention and contract (voluntary adherence), we spontaneously identify morality and some disinterested (not flatly egoistic) pursuit of universal (not flatly particular) objectives, and we can say that even when they take the form of a criticism of Kant, modern political theories in reality succeed as little in finishing off Kant as they do Rousseau.

We need to locate the *Doctrine of Right* in relation to this ethical requirement of universality as described in the *Critique of Practical Reason*. Kant designates the *Doctrine* in a general way by the expression "metaphysics of morals," an expression that surely deserves some explanation. The term "metaphysical" has three quite distinct meanings for Kant and denotes three completely different disciplines:

(*a*) "General metaphysics" is a logical analysis of the traditional concepts of ontology: being, nothing, substance, accident, and so on. Kant grants little interest to it.

(*b*) "Special metaphysics" is the metaphysics whose illusions Kant was determined to attack concerning the absolute subject, completed science, and the existence of God.

(*c*) The "metaphysics of morals" (or nature, which will be disregarded here) refers to the perfectly legitimate procedure by which one thinks of the relation between the universal and the particular. Let us try to be clear:[43] pure morality tells us that we should aim for the universal, but does not tell us what the universal is, merely describing its disembodied form (the reason why it is endlessly repeated that Kant's morality is formalistic). The goal of the *Metaphysics of Morals* and of its first part, the *Doctrine of Right,* is to begin to embody this formal requirement by giving it a minimum of empirical content. To the moral law aiming at the universal is added first the existence of things in general and then that of persons—and it is this addition that determines the main division of the *Doctrine of Right* into private right and public right or, if you will, social right and governmental right.[44]

Let us explain the reasoning further: to understand the principle, one should keep in mind the idea that the quest for the universal is indissolubly linked to human freedom, of which it is the sign, as it were; in seeking the universal, I display my distinctively human (nonanimal) ability to abstract from egoism and hence to free myself from mechanical (causal) determinations. This much is still formal, however. The more concrete question of right appears when I wonder how to perform the free search for the universal in the face of the existence of persons and things. Hence the two central questions of the *Doctrine of Right:*

(*a*) What things (and under what circumstances) can I use freely? This is a question of the right of property or private right that characterizes the sphere of *society.*

(*b*) How can I be free without others being subservient, and, reciprocally, how can others be free without my being subservient? This is a question of public right, coming within the sphere of the state as the place of the right of constraint guaranteeing the reciprocal limitation of freedoms.

Kant's *Doctrine of Right* makes this synthesis of a problematic of morality and one of *jus naturale.* It places law in relation to morality as its embodiment, and, in so doing, it takes empiricity into account and makes possible a purely philosophical distinction between society and the state, the private and the public. It thus seems to us the locus of the shift from natural right, as reflection about legitimacy and sovereignty, to political theory as reflection about the relation between society and state. When this pair is produced, the relations between the two terms of the pair can be considered according to three fundamental modalities:

(1) The reduction of the first term (society) to the second (state), which at the level of philosophical principles grounds the project for governmental, even totalitarian, *socialism* in which the state becomes the authority with a claim to the organization, control, and eventual absorption of the society.

(2) The reduction of the second term to the first, which still at the level of principles grounds the *anarchist* project of totally eliminating the state in favor of a society presumed to be harmonious because it is thought of by analogy with the living organism.

(3) The reciprocal limitation of the two terms, which grounds the *liberal* suspicion that their coincidence is impossible, and that the aim of absolute unity will eventually prove inevitably catastrophic.

Clearly our task was not to "deduce" modern political theories in all their diversity, but merely to indicate how, on the basis of a common adherence to the *subjectivist* presuppositions of the theory of *jus naturale,* three *models* of political theory are set up when the society-state contrast is posited as the central object of political philosophy. The idea of human rights in general makes its first appearance with the theory of *jus naturale.* With political theory, three types of discourse prove possible at the level of principles about the different types of human rights:

(*a*) a liberal discourse that reduces human rights to permissions and sees in them the bases for a limitation of the state;

(*b*) a Marx-inspired socialist discourse that makes entitlements and hence state intervention a prerequisite for the possible actualization of permissions, posited as secondary in the strict sense;

(*c*) an anarchist discourse that attacks these two types of rights as somehow presupposing the state.

Returning to the question asked by Villey concerning the coherence of the modern doctrines of human rights, we need to take up two problems that form a genuine antinomy:

(1) Because permissions seem to be inseparable from a liberal view of the division between society and state, we must first examine their treatment in the Marxist and anarchist criticisms of the 1789 Declaration of the Rights of Man.

(2) But it also behooves us to address the reciprocal question of the status of entitlements in liberal political theories.

Thus, the analysis of these three types of discourse should clear up the antinomy of permissions and entitlements, and we can thus determine to what extent this antinomy can or cannot be resolved, or, if you will, to what extent the idea of human rights is or is not contradictory.

Human Rights and Three Political Theories: Anarchism, Socialism, and Liberalism

The analysis proposed here of the three political theories of modernity makes no claim to exhaustiveness about any of them. Our purpose in the three cases is to explore only their kinds of relation to the discourse of human rights and, when a positive reference is made to human rights, to their capacity for grounding the practice of this reference in reason. In this and only this sense, the relation of these political theories to the discourse of human rights can serve as a guiding principle for testing their internal cohesion.

For each of these theories, our chosen starting point is the positions their representatives adopted about the Revolution of 1848. Two main reasons determined this choice:

(1) As we recalled in our introduction, it was in 1848, during the debates in the National Assembly about the inscription of the right to work in the constitution, that the distinction between entitlements and permissions came to the fore. As we shall see, it was precisely the position adopted on this distinction, and on the relation between these two types of "rights," that was the source of the debates between the anarchists, the socialists, and the liberals. The Revolution of 1848 thus provided the occasion that made this division possible along clearly defined lines of force.[1]

(2) Furthermore, aside from these oppositions, the Revolution of 1848 saw the emergence—out of the disputes between liberals and socialists—of a quite fragile alliance around the idea of a republic:[2] the republican reference seemed to function as a synthetic term making it possible to get beyond the rivalries that emerge in connection with the interpretation of the legacy of the original revolution in France. If, as Raymond Aron suggested,[3] we admit that there is a singular anal-

ogy in many respects between this period of political history (1848–51) and the present day (if only through the debates between socialists and liberals, to say nothing of the anarchistic resurgences appearing in some "libertarian" streams of thought), couldn't we push the analogy further? Couldn't the idea of a republic, with a significance and status to be spelled out, once again offer the synthetic term that can give substance to a true consensus? And if we grant, which is not too difficult, that the idea of a republic was and surely still can be defined through the privileged reference accorded the principles of 1789, we may glimpse how the discourse of the declarations could finally function as a real point of unification around the republican synthesis (thus of a certain interpretation of human rights).

This presupposes, however, that we preliminarily avoid any interpretation of this discourse which might efface its veritably consensual reach and which, moreover, might prevent it from having a true foundation. From this point of view, it also seemed to us fruitful to undertake a critical analysis of anarchist, socialist, and liberal references to the theme of human rights. This critical analysis is carried out in two steps whose presentation may be disconcerting. Thus we indicate briefly their principle:

(*a*) We have included the analyses of the anarchist and Marxist positions in the same chapter: as was noted at the conclusion of part 1, both cases involve arguments against the very distinction between society and the state—according to a symmetrical inverse movement: because Marx condemns the autonomization of the civil society in relation to the state (the separation of human rights and the rights of the citizen) in bourgeois society and subjects the civil society itself to the principle of common interest of which the state claims to become the instrument, it is thus a matter *in this sense,* of reducing the society to the state, reincorporating the civil in the political, thus allowing the state to disappear as a distinct sphere of society. For Proudhon, the problem is one of eliminating the state as such, of contesting the very principle of what claims to embody the will of all, in short, of dissolving the state in the only true place of power, to wit, the society in its diversity. In both cases, the project is thus to abolish the separation between society and state: from this point of view, the two efforts appear to us to be combinable; it is also from this point of view that they seem to us to contain certain potentialities for totalitarianism, if it is admitted that totalitarianism is defined at the very least by the negation of the distinction between society and state.

(*b*) We then examine the liberal position starting with what differentiates it from the project common to anarchism and Marxism; far from abolishing the distinction between society and state, here it is primarily a matter of protecting it—the reason why the reference to human right must in principle be activated. As we shall see, the whole problem is to determine whether liberalism does not also run into formidable difficulties in giving a real meaning and function to these human rights to which it refers in a constitutive way.

The Division of Society and the State as a Problem: Anarchist and Marxist Criticisms of Human Rights

1. Proudhon's Analysis of the Declarations of the Rights of Man

We are acquainted with the general principle guiding all of Proudhon's political thinking, that is, the desire to shift the terrain of the struggle for human emancipation. Through his reserved and even critical attitude toward the Republican party during the whole Second Empire, he expressed a constant conviction, beyond the fluctuations of circumstance:[1] the problem is not one of reconquering the state to use it to resolve the social problem, but of bringing about a "dissolution of political powers" (*C*, 4:156). Hence the successive polemics against the republicans, whom he accused of displaying a "governmental spirit pushed to the point of the fiercest dictatorship" (*C*, 4:11). Hence also a radical criticism of the idea of democracy, one figure, among others, of the "principle of authority": "We have thrust upon the world our supreme idea, the idea of freedom: democracy hasn't heard" (*C*, 3:100)—since through its confidence in the state and through the predominance granted to politics over the economy, the democratic tradition would constitute, according to a letter of 1850, merely "a new stimulus given to Jacobinism" (*C*, 3:144). Two major theses pervade Proudhon's writings:

(1) "Government, at its highest degree of perfection, is organized to effect the subjection and despoilment of the greatest number" (*C*, 4:158): consequently it is no use now to seek "governmental theories"; rather, it is necessary to dissociate the idea of social order and that of government.[2]

(2) "For the system of political power, we have to substitute a system of economic forces," the economic organization needs to replace the "governmental prejudice" to lead societies "to the higher world of humanitarian right" (*OC*, 2:11, n. 4): of course, "this system,

or rather this balance of economic forces, cannot be created through authority" but must "come about through the citizens' implied or expressed consent, that is, through the *free contract*" (*C,* 4:159, Dec. 1851).

We shall return to Proudhon's conception of the "social constitution" (in contrast to the "political constitution") and to what grounds it, to wit, the confidence granted to the interplay of economic interests, posited as spontaneously created "solidarity." But we should first determine to what discourse on human rights this attempt to negate the political gives rise.[3] Because the social revolution, which Proudhon considers inscribed in the "logic of humanity" (*C,* 3:259, 18 May 1850 to C. Langlois), is supposed to lead to "the higher world of humanitarian right," this conviction presupposes some thinking about human rights and the modalities of their actualization. To locate this thinking, we need to spell out Proudhon's critique of democracy, whose generative principles the declarations had attempted to define.

Proudhon's hostility toward democracy is directed as much against the representative system as it is at the democratic principle itself. By echoing Rousseau's criticism of representation, Proudhon first denounces the "mystification of universal suffrage" as a simple trick of the "governmental mind" that allows a power, conferred with authority by election, to believe itself legitimate in "procuring the people's good despite the people"; in this sense universal suffrage, "the surest way to get the people to lie" by speaking in its name, makes democracy "the idea of the state extended ad infinitum" (*OC,* 2:54). Nor does Proudhon's criticism spare the ideal of a direct democracy—and here he differs from Rousseau or, more precisely, he opposes Rousseau to Rousseau. For Rousseau certainly saw that the principle of a social order compatible with freedom lies in the notion of *contract;* but in fact, defining the contract less as "the agreement between man and man" than as "the agreement between the citizen and the government," Rousseau "has not understood anything of the social contract":[4] while the idea of a contract should exclude that of government, Rousseau drew from it an idea of sovereignty such that the particular wills accept to abdicate their freedom to it in favor of a general will to which nothing more could be opposed to prevent tyranny. Consequently, even if the people voted on all laws directly, what is then called popular sovereignty—which is in fact merely the sovereignty of number (for Proudhon says it is unlikely that unanimity will most often prevail—is just a new form of oppression that in turn deserves to be denounced; "Do numbers provide your mind with something more rational, more authentic, more moral than faith or force?" (*OC,* 2:209). Against Rousseau, it is thus necessary to rule out any idea of a *political* expression of the general will in the form of a ballot, whether it is to elect representatives or even to establish a law: "The law of the people, obtained through the ballot, is of necessity a law produced by chance, and the power of the people, established on numbers, is necessarily the power of brute force" (*OC,* 2:227). This critique of the political practice of universal suffrage thus entails a resolute rejection of democracy: "No more government! . . . Neither monarchy, nor aristocracy, not even democracy, if this third term imply some type of government acting in the name of the people and calling itself the people. No authority, no government, even a popular one: that is the Revolution"—in other words, "the organization of economic forces under the supreme law of the contract" (*OC,* 2:199). And, at this level (economic, and not political), Proudhon finds himself close to Rousseau and makes the contractualist principle, that is, the agreement between associated producers (on the basis of an exchange of services), the foundation of the social order in small organizations: just as Rousseau imagined the possibility of a true control by each person over public affairs only in small republics, Proudhon, dreading an increase of the organs needed to guarantee social order in large states, established as the first basis of "all constitutional science" the project "of forming small groups, respectively sovereign, and of uniting them by a pact of federation."[5] Once, against Rousseau himself, the level at which the contractualist idea must be applied is redefined, it becomes possible to defend the practice of universal suffrage, which is certainly to be condemned as a principle of *political* life but uncircumventable as a principle of *social* existence: "In its concept, universal suffrage is the social potential or collective force of the nation in its inaugural form and already active in its functions, that is, in full exercise of its sovereignty" (*OC,* 13:83)—meaning *social sovereignty.* It is precisely to preserve the *social* fruitfulness of universal suffrage (as the unique means of the "management of affairs" in the "whole system of the future society") that its impoverishment must be denounced where it is reduced to "the citizen's prerogative" to "come, every three, five and six years, to choose between various surnames": it is thus a matter of defending universal suffrage against the *political* deviation by which it becomes synonymous with "the periodically renewed resignation of the sovereign people" (*OC,*

13:84). Hence Proudhon's insistence on distinguishing, despite their "apparent synonymy," between a republic and a democracy, the two notions certainly presupposing a valorization of universal suffrage, but from quite different perspectives: while the republican principle defines the social order as the one in which the citizens associate on the basis of an equality of rights, and deliberate in universal suffrage about the management of their affairs, democracy consists in making election by universal suffrage the principle of the subjection of all groups to a unique administration: in this sense democracy represents a political degeneration of the idea of a republic.[6]

In the course of this insistent dialogue with Rousseau[7] upon themes (particularly the contractualist idea) which Rousseau had supposedly deflected from their deepest consequences even as he gave them an unprecedented development, Proudhon is obviously led to evaluate the contribution of what in many respects appeared to him to be inherited from Rousseau's thinking—to wit, the French Revolution and chiefly the Declarations of the Rights of Man. Two essential points need to be stressed here:

(1) According to Proudhon, the Revolution of 1789 and, correspondingly, that of 1848 were correct in proclaiming that "forgetting the rights of man or holding them in contempt are the only causes of public misfortune and of the corruption of governments."[8] This was even "as decisive a way to proceed as it was rational," eventually producing that break with antiquity that Christianity was unable to make. The ancient world had withheld in two ways the assumption of the principle of human dignity; on the one hand, by reducing de facto the dignity of man to "patrician dignity" (*OC,* 1:369); on the other hand, by getting respect from each person for the right of others only by the circuitous route of religion and fear of divine punishment: "If it is maintained that God alone should declare the law, guarantee it, and obtain its observance," then "everyone's feeling toward his own rights does not become respect of the rights of others except as an effect of religion"—in which case "we are bound to follow the principle to its logical consequences, and say that Justice is within us a pretension without basis, and man the divinity's vassal" (*OC,* 1:366). Thus if "man is to create law and 'do right' by man" (*OC,* 1:366), divine determination of right must be avoided, which Christianity was unable to do by committing "the error of renewing the transcendental hypothesis." Far from "saving human dignity" (*OC,* 1:392), the Christian world has, by means of the theme of the fall, even humiliated the human: "Before anything else, the Christian must recognize

his indignity, he must lower himself before his God," and it's in that sense that "Christianity, in its principle, in all its theology, is the condemnation of the human self, in its contempt for the person" (*OC*, 1:397). This contempt for the human doomed Christianity to be one day rejected by human conscience: "A doctrine which transgresses against humanity could not eternally possess humanity" (*OC*, 1:400). And it is up to the Revolution eventually to reject the ancient conception of right and its perpetuation by Christianity; if, "everywhere the religious idea survives," the idea of the just is established "against humanity" (*OC*, 407), the Revolution needed to be carried out first against religion to shift the locus of evil "from the inside" (the selfishness of fallen man) to the "outside" (the disgrace of governments). Hence the virtue of "the set of declarations": even when they placed themselves "under the invocation of the Supreme Being," the declarations do not get the principle of justice from God but from man, who becomes "the subject of justice, its principle, its rules, its sanction"—so much that, for the first time, right appears genuinely as "the right of man vis-à-vis man," that is, as a "right to respect" (*OC*, 1:413).

(2) This hailing of the French Revolution in no way prevents Proudhon from judging that the Declarations of the Rights of Man did not achieve a fully satisfactory conception of human rights. For if the right of man is the "right to respect," "who will determine, in the heart, this respect"? Where the "ancient lawgiver" replied: "the fear of God," the "modern innovators" invoke "the interest of society" (*OC*, 1:413), here repeating the gesture of the ancients (and of Christianity) that consisted in "locating the cause of respect, starting with the principle of right and of justice, outside man"; thereby one thus goes on "denying this very principle," since one destroys "its innateness, immanence, condition sine qua non"; man is not respected for himself, man *as such*—justice reduces "to obedience or utility: it is a fiction."[9] It is thus necessary to go beyond the spirit of the Declarations of the Rights of Man and ground the "right of man vis-à-vis man" on the "immanent and real" principle that Proudhon thinks is found in true justice, to wit, that sovereign faculty, constitutive of man insofar as he feels *solidarity* with the other members of the same collectivity.[10] For human rights not to be a simple fiction, for them not to be the rights of selfishness,[11] it is necessary to escape the bad individualism that animates the declarations of rights and can perfectly lead to a new despotism (that of a coalition of majority interests); for it

not to be "in vain" that "the Revolution . . . had posited the right of man and citizen by its first act," another revolution must "begin a new age for humanity"—a revolution in which men, experiencing their sociability and finally perceiving it as their true dignity, "forming a group," "ipso facto declare the identity and solidarity of their respective dignities, mutually and by the same token recognize each other as sovereign, and bear themselves guarantors of each other" (*OC*, 1:419).

Genuine recognition of human rights would thus involve the principled affirmation of humanity as a collective being, each member of which respects in his fellow only the other member of the same whole and thus respects only himself.[12] Thus is transcended the abstract individualism which, because it separates the individual and the social, cannot recognize "the personality and the autonomy of the masses."[13] This transcendence then has two consequences:

(1) On the strictly political level, this new foundation for human rights implies the very principle of anarchism, that is, the negation of government and the state: because true respect for human dignity appears only in the form of the *spontaneous* agreement of man with man through the mutual recognition of their membership in the same collective being, the organization of a society based on this respect, far from having to be imposed by a government, proceeds only from this sentiment of joint membership: the dissolution of the government in the *social organism* becomes possible when the individual sees that his true dignity lies in solidarity of interests.

(2) As for the content of human rights, Proudhon's procedure imposes certain movements in the course of which anarchism appears rather close to Marx's criticisms: if the spirit of the Declarations of the Rights of Man is judged to be abstract individualism, it is clear that one will be led to find the stamp of this individualism in the letter of the texts of 1789 or 1793; one will thus denounce, as did Marx in *The Jewish Question,* the proclamation of certain rights—and in the first place, the right to property—as incompatible with the real idea of human dignity: making private property the "basis of the social state" is to recognize the legitimacy of an "inequality of conditions" that destroys any possibility of a real "association." With property and inequality, the "social sentiment" of solidarity disappears: the "right of the poor" will be the opposite of the "usurpation of the rich," the society will be maintained only by the force of the rich trying to hold onto their wealth—in short, the recognition of

the right to property leads to despotism and hence to the negation of human dignity.[14] If we intend to ground the respect for human rights in the sentiment of human solidarity ("the love of self in others"), it is thus proper to posit, pace the Declaration of 1789, that "equality of condition is a necessary consequence of natural right . . . and of the very principle of society" (*OC*, 4:310)—meaning "equality of *means*, not equality of *well-being*, which with equal means must be the work of the laborer" (*OC*, 4:342). Just as Proudhon defends, against the first declarations and in anticipation of the history of entitlement rights, the thesis that human rights, which are to enable man to exist as such, must first enable him to *live*, hence to satisfy certain needs: "it's a need to eat and sleep: it's a right to provide ourselves with the things necessary for sleep and nourishment" (*OC*, 4:343). In a word: for the content of human rights to be in harmony with that which establishes their wide acceptance and not shatter, but rather favor, social solidarity, the declarations need to be completed in the direction of a recognition of certain rights without which the rights already proclaimed would remain fictive or, if you will, formal.

This convergence between the anarchist redefinition of the content of the declarations and the theme, central to the socialist tradition, of the recognition of entitlements, should clearly not be taken too far: Proudhon is not trying to get the state to take on the responsibility for actualizing the rights thus redefined. The important *Lettres aux ouvriers* concerning the elections of 1864 (*OC*, vol. 13) clearly disapproves of the initiative of the *Manifeste des soixante,* by the engraver Tolain, who justified the worker candidacies in the hope of using political means to achieve social emancipation: beyond a criticism of the existing political and electoral system, Proudhon primarily stresses that "all these systems are equally valid" and that "it would be absurd to express some preference"—for as soon as there is a government the people are no longer sovereign and human dignity (human rights) is scorned. Thus it is not a matter of capturing the power of the state so that the government, not limited to guaranteeing formal rights, will take responsibility for social rights: on the contrary, in the very name of human dignity, the state and all principle of authority must be abolished in such a way as to bring about that anarchy "in which the public and private conscience alone . . . suffices for the maintenance of order and the guarantee of all freedoms." It is "when political life and domestic existence become identical that, all constraint having disappeared . . . the social law will be carried out by itself, without supervision or command, in universal spontaneity" (*OC*, 13:131, letter of 20 August 1864). Thus, it is necessary above all to defend human rights *against the state,* and that while facing up to both liberals and socialists at the same time:

—Liberals suffer from the illusion of a possible limitation of the state, but as soon as state power exists, it tends of itself to unlimitation: in this sense, anarchism posits itself as the truth of a too naïve liberalism concerning the state.[15]

—Socialists believe in the possible use of the state for the full establishment of popular sovereignty, but as soon as a state exists, the people are dispossessed of their rights: to socialism anarchism opposes the "absolute incompatibility of power and freedom."[16]

2. The Totalitarian Presuppositions of Anarchist Discourse

The great themes of the anarchist criticism of the state are relatively well known—and we have seen how they inescapably led Proudhon to make a radical criticism of human rights for implying the presence of the state. The core of Proudhon's argumentation explicitly lies in the idea that there is basically more continuity than rupture between the political theories originating in the French Revolution and the absolutist doctrine in force during the ancien régime: in each case political authority is certainly assigned a different origin and legitimacy, but in both cases its very principle is not called into question: "The ancien régime, based upon authority and faith, was in essence that of divine right. The principle of popular sovereignty which was later added to it did not in any way change its nature; it is in error that today . . . some wish to maintain, between absolute and constitutional monarchy, between the latter and the democratic republic, a distinction which in no way affects its principle" (*GIR,* 282).[17] Hence the common rejection, already noted, as much of the obvious forms of absolutism as of its disguised forms, such as "direct government and direct legislation . . . the two biggest blunders talked about in the annals of politics and philosophy" (*GIR,* 113).[18]

The question immediately raised by this all-out attack on the state is the one that Proudhon himself asks in *Idea of a Revolution:* what is to be put in the "place of the government," and, we add, on what philosophical basis are we to see the hypotheses of its elimination as *obvious?* That is, how do we go from "negative anarchy" to "positive anarchy" that must finally yield the principle of a nongovernmental social organization?

Proudhon gives his answer in one of the interminable enumerations he is fond of:

> What we replace the government with . . . is industrial organization.
> What we replace the laws with are contracts . . .
> What we replace political power with are economic forces.
> What we replace the old classes of citizens with . . . are the categories and specializations of functions: agriculture, industry, commerce, etc.
> What we replace public force with is collective force.
> What we replace standing armies with are industrial companies.
> What we replace the police with is the identity of interests.
> What we replace political centralization with is economic centralization.(*GIR,* 284)

Each aspect of this positive anarchy warrants comment. To confine ourselves to the main point, we immediately see that the founding principle of nongovernmental social organization is the idea that, thanks to a certain conception of the social contract that remains to be spelled out, politics can be definitively replaced by economics— an illusion common to Saint-Simon, Marx, and Proudhon.[19] For Proudhon, only the idea of a contract makes it possible to conceive of a nonhierarchical social organization, a social organization from "bottom to top" that will be called, depending on the level considered, mutualism, communalism, or federalism.

It should be recalled that the anarchist contract is opposed not only to the notion of hierarchy, but also to that of association: "I have always looked upon association as upon an equivocal commitment which, like pleasure, love, and many other things, encloses, inside a most seductive appearance, more bad than good" (*GIR,* 83)—an assertion by which Proudhon opposes a whole aspect of the nineteenth-century utopian tradition. For the idea of association must be substituted by that of *reciprocity,* which presupposes a free and rational commitment on the part of the contracting parties. The social contract must be "synallagmatic" and "commutative" such that each contracting party has more to gain that to lose, though it remains completely free, "less what is relative to the special object for which the contract is formed." Thus it is such a contract that, reproduced an unlimited number of times in the course of each individual agreement, it must constitute the true keystone of the federalist structure.

It clearly appears that, aside from the disappearance of the state, this contract is in principle directed at the complete reduction of the political to the economic when we consider, if only briefly, its implied criticism of Rousseau's social contract. This criticism primarily concerns two points.

(1) Proudhon attacks Rousseau's social contract for tending to reinforce political power by legitimating it—an operation Proudhon sees as resulting from the confusion of government and the general will (?), though in truth "the idea of a contract excludes that of government" (*GIR,* 124).

(2) But secondly—and this is without any doubt the most important—Rousseau's social contract is suspected of radically disregarding the concrete life of society, that is, the economic life: "Not a word about work, or property, or the industrial forces the organization of which is the task of the social contract. . . . His program is exclusively political; he acknowledges only political rights, he does not acknowledge economic rights" (*GIR,* 131).

We thus see that the true significance of Proudhon's social contract is economic: "Commutative justice, the law of contracts; *in other words,* the industrial or economic regime: such are the different synonyms of the idea whose advent should abolish the old systems" (*GIR,* 124). The great virtue of communism, which Proudhon cannot avoid hailing, is to see that "instead of splitting politics and political economy, as does the bourgeois system, and making two distinct and contrary orders," one must affirm "the identity of their principles and try to make a synthesis of them," so true is it that "economic unity" is "destined by the progress of ideas to replace political unity," that is, in Proudhon's inimitable style: "Between the political regime and the economic regime, between the regime of laws and the regime of contracts, no possible fusion, we must choose: the ox, if it goes on being an ox, cannot become an eagle, nor the bat a snail. In the same way if society keeps, to whatever degree, its political form, it cannot organize itself according to the economic law" (*GIR,* 282).

The ultimate presupposition of the critique of the state then appears in full clarity: what is literally postulated by Proudhon's anarchism and which constantly comes through even in the metaphors he uses is that the state is a *dead* artifact, while society, revealed to itself, is harmonious because it is analogous to a *living* being: that is why "it cannot be a matter of working on society itself, which we must consider to be a superior being endowed with its own life and which in consequence rules out on our part any notion of arbitrary reconstitution" (*GIR,* 80).

Political philosophy often employs metaphors of the organism. Proudhon, however, chooses the most disastrous of them: that of life. As Philonenko[20] has shown, in modern thought, the organism is conceived of according to three models:

(1) The mechanical model—as we see in Cartesianism (and, in a sense, in contemporary molecular biology!)—reduces the organism to a machine, an automaton, certainly sublimely advanced but still reducible to solely mechanistic laws.

(2) The model of the organized being that is not yet the living being and of which the typical example is the plant. What characterizes the organized being—which Kant's *Critique of Judgment* describes *in this sense* for the first time—is the fact that its individuality is still merely *relative:* we can consider, for example, a tree as *an* individual, but we can also in turn consider each branch of this tree an individual, for a branch can be grafted onto another tree, or even simply planted in the ground. The transposition of this model to the political sphere has quite remarkable properties: for example, when we conceive of the social contract as analogous to a graft by which individuals are incorporated into a common trunk, the metaphor clearly suggests that each individual in the social whole thus constituted remains an autonomous being, independent of the other (the way the branch is, if you will, independent of the tree that bears it). The whole does not absorb the parts.

(3) This is what takes place at the level of life (which is not to be confused with organization): life is the domain of *absolute* individuality in the sense that the articulated members of a living being (and not just its organs) can have no separate existence, unlike the branches of a tree. Comparing the political body to a living being is thus to suggest that individuals (the members) have no autonomous existence and that the whole absorbs the parts that it encompasses and, ultimately, allows to exist.

The theme of society without the state is not without its dangers. The analysis of Proudhon's criticism of human rights provides us with yet another proof of this. In claiming to eliminate the division between society and state in favor of a "vitalistic" conception of social organization, Proudhon sets, to our minds, anarchist thinking on a path leading to totalitarianism—which had been already foreshadowed by the theme of a liquidation of the political in favor of the economic.

With the inverse symmetrical presuppositions, for it tends, at least at first, to increase the state's control over society, the Marxist critique of human rights also leads to problematical conclusions through its aim to eliminate the division between society and state.

3. The Marxist Critique of Human Rights

Because the great themes of this critique are well known, we shall be brief.[21] Marx's analysis of the Declaration of the Rights of Man must of course be situated in the general framework of the interpretation of the "bourgeois revolution." We know how for Marx this revolution ended up producing a state separate from civil society, a state that, by taking on the appearance of aiming at the universal, is in reality merely a tool for giving free rein to particular (capitalistic) interests in society: "Through the emancipation of private property from the community, the State has become a separate entity, beside and outside civil society; but it is nothing more than the form of organisation which the bourgeois necessarily adopt both for internal and external purposes, for the mutual guarantee of their property and interests."[22] It is in this perspective that Marx's careful but—as we shall see— selective examination, in *The Jewish Question,* of the various declarations of human rights is situated. Straightaway, he stresses how the famous distinction between *man* and *citizen* by which a level, that of the citizen, is isolated at which the requirement of universality can be affirmed, in reality occurs only to guarantee the free interplay of private interests that continue to rule the relations among men. As Jürgen Habermas wrote: "Marx comprehends the bourgeois revolution as the emancipation of citizens [burghers] but not of human beings: recognized before the law as free and equal legal persons, still at the same time the citizens are at the mercy of the natural conditions of a society of exchange, which has been set free."[23] Despite, or rather because of, the generosity of its proclaimed intentions, bourgeois society thus remains an in-principle selfish society, oriented to private profit and based on the balance of power that tends to isolate individuals from each other: "It is just the striving of independent individuals and their wills, which on this basis are necessarily egoistic in their behavior toward each other, which makes self-denial through law and regulation essential, or rather self-denial in exceptional cases and maintenance of their interest in general"[24]— the reason why in his discussion of the declaration of human rights Marx detects in the statement of each of the human rights the selfishness that they both set free and cover over.

Thus, for example, in article 6 of the Constitution of 1793, the definition of freedom as "the power that belongs to man to do anything that does no harm to the rights of others," indicates the monadic nature of the individual in bourgeois civil society: "Liberty is, therefore, the fight to do everything which does not harm others. The limits within which each individual can act without harming others are determined by law, just as the boundary between two fields is marked by a stake. It is a question of the liberty of man regarded as an isolated monad, withdrawn into himself." [25] And in the subsequent part of his discussion of article 6, Marx stresses how the real meaning of this definition of freedom lies in its purely negative character in the fact that it does *not* establish relations between men, but on the contrary allows free play for their separation and even antagonism. Under the requirement of security, which according to article 8 of the Constitution of 1795 lies "in the protection granted by society to each of its members for the preservation of his person, his rights and property," is according to Marx—another example of his "genealogical" reading—"the supreme concept of bourgeois society, the concept of the police" that must be brought to light, such that "through the concept of security, bourgeois society does not rise above its selfishness," but on the contrary finds in it its surest guarantee. [26] Giving each of the permissions the same treatment, Marx can conclude that this "man as distinct from the *citizen*," who "is no other than the member of bourgeois society," is "selfish man," "man separated from man and the collectivity." [27]

A brilliant analyst of the Revolution of 1848, Marx thus opted unreservedly to defend entitlements not only next to permissions but, one can say, *against* them, so great was his contempt for parliamentary institutions and, more generally, public freedoms. And it is of course the right to work, inscribed in the first project for a constitution written before the days of June, that benefits before all else from his consent: "The right to work is, in the bourgeois sense, nonsense, a wretched, pious wish. But behind the right to work stands power over capital, the appropriation of the means of production, their subjection to the associated working class, that is the abolition of wage labor, capital, and their mutual relationship." [28] Further on, we shall see how close this analysis is to Tocqueville's—although, need we point out, their evaluations of the right to work are radically opposed. It is important merely to note that Marx's criticism of permissions is logically inscribed in the project for establishing the total domination of the state over society. In his article "Politics and Human Rights," Claude Lefort gives what we find to be a brilliant demonstration that this project has, at least potentially, totalitarian implications.[29]

According to Lefort—and how can we not follow him here?—though in the totalitarian regimes of the East "man is dissociated from man and separated from the community as he never was in the past ... it is not because he is assigned to the limits of a private life, to the status of the monad, because he enjoys the right to have opinions, freedoms, property and security, but because this enjoyment is forbidden."[30] Thus Lefort raises three seemingly irrefutable objections to Marx's interpretation of the declarations:

—First, he criticizes Marx for allowing himself to be caught in the trap of bourgeois ideology and making a superficial reading of the declarations by sticking to appearances: "Marx falls into and draws us into a trap which, on other occasions and for other purposes, he was very skillful in dismantling: that of ideology. He allows himself to become the prisoner of the ideological version of rights, without examining what they mean in practice, what profound changes they bring to social life."[31]

—This explains why Marx is forced to pass over in silence the articles of the declarations that are plainly incompatible with his reading in terms of radical selfishness, notably articles 10 and 11 that affirm not only freedom of opinion but also "the free *communication* of thoughts and opinions": "Was Marx so obsessed by his schema of the bourgeois revolution that he could not see that freedom of opinion is a freedom of relationships, that it is man's right, one of his most precious rights, to step out of himself and to make contact with others through speech, writing and thought,"[32] in short, to overlook the fact that the declarations create the possibility of a true "public space" whose impact transcends by far the supposed interests of the bourgeoisie?

—Finally, and this is the main point, Lefort very soundly attacks the assumption that the rights mentioned in the declarations are purely formal and ahistorical—a formalism and ahistoricity that obviously mark the very concrete and historical interests of the bourgeois class. This argument, on which the Marxist distinction between formal and real rights is based, is strangely reminiscent of those already mobilized by the most reactionary thinkers about the French Revolution: it lacks the idea, which is central to a real understanding of the purpose of human rights, that a certain "indetermination" is indispensable to their critical impact. It is because they have a universal and hence abstract aim that these rights can serve, even today, as reference points for social and political struggles whose historical reality can be quite diverse: "Once the rights of man are declared, there arises, so it is said, the fiction of man without determination. The entire critique of Marxist inspiration, but also the conservative critique, rushes into that fragile citadel and demolishes it. Thus Joseph de Maistre declared: 'I have met Italians, Russians, Spaniards, Englishmen, Frenchmen, but I do not know Man'; and Marx thought that there were only concrete individuals, historically and socially determined, shaped by their class condition. With less talent, a number of our contemporaries continue to sneer at abstract humanism." [33]

If neither anarchism nor Marxism manages to give a coherent status to permissions, that is because, impelled by the project of a real suppression of the division between society and state, they are also abolishing the main condition of possibility for these rights. Though liberalism, as a theory of the limits of the state, seems the natural place for these permissions, it is still uncertain whether the foundation it gives them is itself free of all difficulty. As we suggested in the introduction, liberal thinking, from the outset, is pervaded by what could be called an "economistic" and historicist tendency already detectable in the American "founding fathers" and also to some extent in French liberalism, and which comes back today with surprising clarity, or should we say naïveté, in the neoliberalism of a Hayek, in the form of a claim to make a literal deduction of the legal from the economic. On the other hand, it is clear that liberalism—and this too since its origins—adopts a position of radical hostility to the second path of human rights, entitlements. Thus we now have to question the liberal tradition about its attitude toward the two types of human rights.

The Division of Society and
the State as a Value:
Liberalism and Human Rights

Although the liberal tradition, whatever its various inflections from
Constant to the present day, is always defined by the refusal to reconcile society and state in a way that presupposes the disappearance
of one of the two terms, it is clear that to guarantee the difference or
distance between the majority of the members of the society and the
minority wielding power, that is, the state apparatus, the liberal tradition has to accentuate an insurmountable "brake" that can avoid
the risks of a total (totalitarian) confusion between the civil and the
political. We know how, even before the American and French declarations in the eighteenth century, through the great English charters
retrospectively called "liberal," a first referece to fundamental rights
that were inviolable by state authority intervened to that end (the
Magna Carta of 1215, the Star Chamber Act of 1640, the Habeas Cor-
pus of 1670, the Bill of Rights of 1689). Thus, as early as 1215, article
28 of the Great Charter of Jean sans Terre proclaimed: "No constable
or other officer of the king shall take corn or other movable goods
from any one without immediate payment, unless the seller freely
accepts postponement." Thus, a prehistory of human rights could
easily be reconstructed[1] that would be strictly parallel to that of the
criticisms of absolutism and the genesis of the liberal theses.[2] The
liberal valorization of the division between society and state implies
the insistent presence, in the liberal tradition, of a discourse about
human rights whose specificity and possible difficulties we would
like to measure here. For that purpose it seemed potentially advis-
able to listen to this discourse at the precise moment its originality
was affirmed relative to other interpretations of human rights—to
wit, as we have already noted, in 1848, at the time of the debates
between socialists and liberals about the possible inclusion of the
right to work in the constitution.

1. Tocqueville's Criticism of the Right to Work

Handily elected to the Constituent Assembly in May 1848,[3] Tocque-ville took an active part in the debate about the right to work that divided the assembly in September of that same year. On 12 September he addressed the chamber with a speech that has the interest of clearly and vigorously locating the question of the right to work in the more general conflict between socialists and liberals (Tocque-ville called them "democrats") concerning the role of the state before society. We should recall that as early as 25 February the provisional government proclaimed the right to work (the archetypical entitlement) and created two institutions to give it some content: under the minister of public works, the National Workshops which were designed to provide work for the unemployed, and the Governmental Commission for the Workers, which was charged with proposing plans for "the organization of work," in the words of Louis Blanc, and for settling certain conflicts between employers and workers. When we add that the "June Days" broke out following some brutal steps against the workshops, which the assembly deemed politically dangerous and economically ineffective, we can understand the emotional and political charge of the September debates.

It was in this context that Tocqueville argued for the rejection of an amendment sponsored by Deputy Mathieu from the Drôme, who wanted to inscribe the right to work in the Constitution of 1848, following, to be honest, the path opened by the proclamations of the provisional government of February. Most of Tocqueville's argumentation is unsurprising: against the demands of socialism, it points up the strictly liberal values of the original French Revolution, and tries to show that to consider state assistance a right must be dangerous and even absurd. What is striking in this speech, however, is the coherence with which it brings out the political implications of inscribing the right to work in the constitution. According to Tocqueville, the implications can lie only in the establishment of communism or socialism.

Here we should quote the reasoning in its near-totality:

> Either the State will undertake to provide all the workers who come to it with the employment they do not have, in which case it is forced, little by little, to become an industrialist; and since it is the manager of industries one finds everywhere, the only one that cannot refuse to offer work . . . it is inevitably led to making itself the chief and, soon, in

> a sense, the only entrepreneur in industry . . . that, however, is communism. If on the other hand the State wishes to escape the fatal necessity I have just spoken of, if it wishes not to give work to all the workers who come to it of itself and with its own resources, but rather to see to it that they find work among private parties . . . it is constrained to see to it that there be no unemployment; that leads it obligatorily to distribute workers so that they do not compete with each other, to regulate wages, to sometimes slow down production, at other times to accelerate it: in a word to make itself the one and only organizer of work,

in which lies the essence of socialism.

We see that Tocqueville's argument is close to that of Marx, who also saw "behind the right to work" the pure and simple disappearance of the contradiction between capital and the salaried classes. One suspects that Tocqueville's diagnosis is poles apart from Marx's, however. In socialism—which he rather flatly defines by three features: the appeal to material passions, the attacks on property, and the tutelary role of the state becoming master of every individual— Tocqueville basically sees the return to an archaic idea in a world that is nonetheless dominated by the equality of the moderns. Just as Constant saw in the Convention a residue of monarchical absolutism, Tocqueville compares socialism and the ancien régime: "In fact, the Ancien Régime professed the opinion that the only wisdom is in the State, that its subjects are weak, invalid creatures whose hand must always be held . . . that it's a good thing to hinder, impede, ceaselessly to restrain individual liberties; that it is necessary to regulate industry, insure the good quality of products, obstruct free competition. On this point the Ancien Régime thought precisely as do the socialists to-day."

So, according to Tocqueville, it is incumbent to return to the tradition of 1789, which sees in state assistance a *moral duty* but no *legal obligation*. Thus, particularly concerning work, it is a matter of "imposing on the state a more extensive, more sacred duty than the one it has imposed on itself up to now," of "increasing, consecrating and regularizing public charity"; but it is necessary to maintain that "there is nothing here that gives the worker a right over the state; there is nothing here that forces the state to take the place of individual foresight, economy, or individual honesty."

Mathieu's amendment was defeated by 596 votes to 146, and to take a close look at it, the Constitution of 1848, in which some have at times thought to find a recognition of entitlements, is actually much closer than it seems on this point to the spirit of 1789 or to the highly liberal Constitution of 1791. Title I of its Preamble, where we read that France proposes "to ensure an increasingly equitable distribution of the burdens and benefits of society," is very cautious—just as its Title VIII, in which the republic commits itself, "through fraternal assistance," only to "ensuring the existence of needy citizens, either by obtaining work for them within the limits of its resources, or by giving, for want of family, help to those unable to work." These formulas cannot in any case be confused with an effective recognition of entitlements; what's more, they are not really new, for we read in the first title of the Constitution of 1791: "A general establishment of *public relief* shall be created and organized, to bring up abandoned children, relieve the invalid poor and provide work to the able-bodied poor who have not been able to obtain it." In short, public charity—but charity is not a right.

Thus, as early as 1848, Tocqueville's speech on the question of the right to work reveals with an unequaled clarity the specificity and logic of the liberal version of a reference to human rights: since the goal of politics is not to produce human happiness in society through the action of the state, but only for the latter to guarantee individuals the *freedoms* to seek what they take to be happiness,[4] the power of the state must be *defined* by a twofold reference to these permissions—both as the unique *telos* of the action of political power (ensuring the protection of this sphere of freedoms) and as the *limit* of that action (beyond this objective, the acceptance of "entitlements" would legitimate the growing intervention of the state in satisfying needs). *Permissions versus entitlements*—the principle of the liberal position is thus fixed: the reference to the lone and authentic human rights (permissions) provides "the rule that makes it possible to determine the boundary between what the state should concern itself with and what it should leave to the free interplay of individual wishes."[5]

As clear and sharp as it is, this liberal interpretation of the theme of human rights seems no less burdened by a number of difficulties that are apt to be forgotten in the return to favor presently enjoyed by the liberal theses—because of the antitotalitarian impact of the reminder of the "limits of the action of the state."[6] We confine ourselves to identifying two of these difficulties, embryonic in Constant and Tocqueville, but made quite explicit in the subsequent liberal tradition, particularly in its current form: on the one hand, the tendency to "disregard the imperative of social justice";[7] on the other hand—according to a logic that is more rarely analyzed and hence deserves a closer look—a singular resurgence of a historicism perhaps as radical as in the Marxist tradition to which liberalism is so often presented as a kind of antidote.

2. The Questioning of Entitlements and the Rejection of Social Justice: François Guizot and the Criticism of Democracy

We shall not analyze the stages of this first shift as it took place from Constant to Guizot.[8] We shall confine ourselves to noting its effect in a short but important text of 1849 in which Guizot points out to the elected president, Louis-Napoléon Bonaparte, the "evil" eroding all freedoms and for which a cure is to be found, to wit, "democratic idolatry." Guizot's *On Democracy in France* attempts to establish that the term "democracy," which "all parties invoke," now conceals "chaos," more exactly, "the chaos of social war" (*DF,* 42). Indeed, Guizot explains in terms inherited from Constant, by bringing to power "the unique will of the numerical majority of the nation," the "democratic republic" inherently tends to despotism in that, claiming to give "all citizens" a share in power, it loses all mistrust of power and fails to set limits to it: "No powers distinct and in and of themselves strong enough to control and contain each other. No solid bulwarks behind which the different rights and interests can install themselves. No organization of guarantees, no counterweight to the center of the State and to the heights of government" (*DF,* 43). In short, when this despotism prevails, the "individual freedoms of the citizens" ("political freedom") are threatened, only "the right to insurrection" (*DF,* 44) remains to oppose to the state—the democratic republic thus taking the risk inherent in all despotisms, that of producing the chaos of "social struggles." Guizot then judges that to preserve "social peace" in the face of this "immense danger," the cunning of democracy then consists in developing "ideas of the social republic": certainly, this despotism of the "numerical majority of the nation" threatens the "individual freedoms of citizens," but this sacrifice will be easily accepted because it is accompanied by the attainment, precisely by the greatest number, of the *happiness* formerly reserved for "certain men, certain families, certain classes" and now proclaimed the object of an "equal right" for "all men." In affirming that "all men have the right, the same right, an equal right to happiness," the social republic (and Guizot is primarily aiming at "Monsieur Proudhon and his friends") denounces any "confiscation" of a "part of the human treasury" in favor of a few as "contrary to right," and claims that each person should "find the good things of life equally accessible": "to ensure universal enjoyment and equal distribution among all men" of the "goods that bring happiness," this is henceforth "the goal that is pursued and that is professed to be obtainable." In short, through the intermediary of the despotism it engenders and to flatter the masses it represents, the democratic republic leads to the social republic that "sees men only as isolated and ephemeral beings," appearing "in life and on this earth, the theater of life, only to obtain subsistence and pleasure, each for his benefit alone, by the same right and without any other end"; on the pretext of affirming a right of *humanity* to happiness, "it is precisely the condition of *animals*" that is created: "Among them no bond, no action which survives individuals and extends to all, no permanent appropriation, no passing on of inheritance ... nothing but individuals who appear and pass away"; in a word: "The social republic abolishes the human race" (*DF*, 59ff.). Faced with this logic of degeneracy, Guizot devotes the last part of his essay to reaffirming that while the abolition of particular civil privileges and rights definitely represented "a new and immense fact in the history of human societies," it is no less true that "identical laws and equal rights" must not exclude, but on the contrary protect "profoundly diverse and unequal social situations" (*DF*, 74): only the recognition of "various classes" as "natural elements" will make "a great step toward social peace" (*DF*, 106), which will be unobtainable as long as a single class (and the party representing it) claims to seize power for its own exclusive benefit. Thus, to avoid destroying the human race through the democratic republic that has become the social republic, "all the conservative forces of society . . . [must] be closely united" to stem the rising flood tide of democracy" (*DF*, 125). To the conserving energy of inequalities must of course be joined a *moral* (and not at all political) assumption of responsibility for the problem of poverty, the true condition of a lasting social peace: "social affairs" are not a matter of "political mechanics," but it is enough to revive "the Christian virtues" of "faith, hope, and charity"—for then "the rich, the great of the earth, would apply themselves with devotion and perseverance to relieving the miseries of other men," and "the poor, for their part, the little people of the earth, would be subject to the wishes of God and the laws of society: they would seek the satisfaction of their needs in regular and assiduous work, the betterment of their fate in moral and provident conduct, their consolation and their hope in the future promised to man elsewhere" (*DF*, 130–31).

Depending on one's temperament, one finds these conclusions meaningful or excruciating. A longer analysis should in any case stress how some themes and motifs already present in Constant (criticism of the general will as despotic) and Tocqueville's *Democracy in America* (the attack on individualism in the democratic countries) are here placed in a light that harshly shows up certain features of liberal thinking: the opposition between permissions and entitlements (the right to happiness) reveals its inadequacy when, based on it, no effort is made to give social rights a precise status that avoids assigning responsibility for them merely to "Christian virtues." In this inability of the liberal tradition to conceptualize entitlements (which it rightly distinguishes from permissions), there is an initial and serious problem of such a discourse about human rights—more generally, a difficulty that reveals what seems to be hopelessly outdated in this political theory: the requirement of social justice "has entered hearts and minds"[9]—a fact whose recognition cannot replace political theory but whose negation makes a theory, however intelligent, hard to reconcile with the very conditions of modernity.

In denouncing its scorn of social justice, one should not, however, underestimate the liberal tradition and its resources: hyperbolical on this point, F. A. Hayek's recent book shows that by taking the dissociation between permissions and entitlements to its extreme, a radical liberalism is harder to criticize than might be thought if one confined oneself to Guizot's writings. On the other hand, through Hayek's strategy in arguing for the elimination of entitlements, a second problem for liberal discourse, concerning its possible compatibility with a reference to human rights (including permissions), is revealed with a particular clarity.

3. The Historicist Dissolution of Permissions: Hayek's Evolutionism

The attention generally accorded Hayek's ideas[10] at the time of the publication of the French translation of *Law, Legislation and Liberty*[11] is surely explained by the challenging nature of a work setting itself up as an antitype to Marxism and the whole socialist tradition. Let us recall the terms of the challenge: the ideal of "social justice" defining the socialist tradition is "wholly illusory," and "any attempt concretely to realize it [is] apt to produce a nightmare" (*LLL*, 2:85)—in short, either you abandon any claim for "equality of material position," any "egalitarian considerations" defining the socialist idea of justice, or you contribute to creating "a totalitarian system in which personal freedom would be absent" (*LLL,* 2:77). Here the separation of permissions and entitlements thus reaches its culmination: in a seemingly symmetrical way to what Marx had attempted in *The Jewish Question* (a critique of permissions as formal rights, in the name of real or material rights, namely, entitlements), Hayek makes a radical critique of material rights, about which he presents any assumption of responsibility as a negation of permissions. Three main theses then bolster this challenge to the values of the socialist tradition.

(1) The denunciation of the "constructivist illusion."

According to Hayek, it is first of all a philosophical tradition beginning with Descartes and Hobbes and including the *Social Contract* that is to be blamed for generating a plan for a voluntary reconstitution of the social order according to the principles of human reason (*LLL,* 1:9ff); by dismissing "tradition, custom, and history in general," this voluntarism sets out to "remodel our society and our institutions" and thus make them conform to "objectives" (to a "plan") whose implementation is supposed to allow for the fulfillment of humanity (*LLL,* 1: ibid.). Politically "perverse" (in giving itself the right to define the rules of a just organization of the social, reason sets itself up as the absolute source of laws and, as such, creates the idea of an unlimited sovereignty in which legislative reason is not subject to anything other than itself), this "constructivist rationalism" rests on a theoretical error, to wit, what Hayek calls "the synoptic illusion," which he attacked as early as 1944 in his criticism of "scientistic totalism." [12] To put it simply, the project of a rational, voluntary, and deliberate reconstruction of the social order, in order not to be absurd, presupposes a subject that is omniscient with regard to society; but an objective knowledge of the totality of social processes is impossible—if only because the knowing subject is itself part of what it seeks an objective total vision of: by definition, it cannot see objectively, hence "from the outside," a totality that it itself belongs to. According to Hayek, the bringing to light of this veritable hermeneutic circle that is constitutive of the social sciences is sufficient to devastate the constructivist conception for which order should be introduced in the social field by a human desire for organization: to this order originating in wills (*taxis*), *Law, Legislation and Liberty* opposes a natural order immanent in the social as such (*cosmos*) that is not to be created but to be discovered and protected; correspondingly, to the laws that constructivist rationalism conceives as the work of men (*thesis* = the established law) is opposed a right inscribed in the very nature of things (*nomos*), a law of which man is not the source but merely the interpreter. To discover these pairs *taxis-cosmos* and *thesis-nomos* is to be tempted to place Hayek next to thinkers like Leo Strauss or Michel Villey who oppose modern natural right with the juridical naturalism of the Greeks: Hayek's criticism of human rights would then be classed with a return to the ancients, whose various problems we have already analyzed. Once again, we should avoid hasty appearances and conclusions—and to spell out what these natural laws and this natural order are for Hayek: they are for him the order and laws of the *market*.

(2) An information-theoretical analysis of the functioning of the market.

Against the unrealistic conception of a market in which consumers and producers adjust supply and demand based on a perfect knowledge of available products and existing needs, Hayek proposes to represent the order of the market (the cosmos of the market) as "catallactic," as proceeding from a continual exchange of information through which the objectives of individuals spontaneously adjust to each other (*LLL,* 2:108ff.). The mechanism of this exchange (*catallaxy*) of information is simple: in the market, each person pursues his own objectives (to buy this or that consumer good, to produce this or that commodity) with no limit on his initiatives other than those of respect for the "the rules of the law of property, tort and contract" (*LLL,* 2:109)—rules whose only function is to protect the spontaneous order of the market and to ensure the self-deployment of its immanent laws. In thus pursuing his own goals, the individual receives certain information from the market about the possible or impossible integration of his plans into the social order: for example, the benefits that his efforts are worth to a producer constitute a sign that informs him that his products contribute to the satisfaction of needs *that he does not know;* the price of the consumer good the buyer covets is an indicator of the compatibility or incompatibility of his desire (depending on whether the price is affordable or not) with the order of the market, that is, with the facts of a production process *that he does not know.* The market functions through this *coded* diffusion of information with no need to shape it from the outside through the intermediary of any planning rationality, the sum of whose knowledge will always be inadequate to do this. Consequently, we understand why Hayek must condemn any state intervention in the order of the market (and hence any mixed economy), in other words, why his liberalism is so *radical:* any intervention would introduce *disorder,* in the cybernetic sense of the term, in the self-regulated "game of catallaxy" that "leads to an increase in the stream of goods and of the prospects of all participants to satisfy their needs" (*LLL,* 2:115). To "intervene" would be to disturb that "wealth-creating game" that makes possible "the satisfaction of a broader range of needs." The result is what Hayek considers "the political order of a free people": if, through the free play of supply and demand, each person obtains a quantity of information that gives direction to economic and social activity better than any *constructed* institution can, the role of the state is merely to create the legal framework for the maximal diffusion of information within the society—thus the framework for the freest development of the game of catallaxy. The state will therefore be primarily the defender of individual freedoms: the sole legitimate power of a government is to preserve the formal rights of the individual as such, "negative rights" whose declaration consists only in prohibiting anyone from prohibiting to the individual the use of his freedoms insofar as they are compatible with those of others.[13] Hayek says that the political error begins when "'social and economic' human rights" are added to these negative rights, these positive rights claiming to determine the material situation that the government *should* provide every individual with: to be satisfiable, these "claims to particular benefits to which every human being as such is presumed to be entitled" (*LLL,* 2:103) presuppose that the constraint exercised by the government, far from limiting itself to getting respect for the freedom of an individual, is organized to determine the material situation of individuals and groups. According to Hayek, this is precisely the source of the totalitarian drift of democracy—that is, the mixture of negative rights and positive rights, freedoms and entitlements, in the discourse of human rights.

(3) A critique of the idea of social justice, paradoxically made in the name of the idea of equality.

In reading *Law, Legislation and Liberty,* not only does this idea appear "probably the gravest threat to most other values of a free civilization,"[14] but Hayek's analysis reduces it to a simple "phantasm" or "mirage." Any appeal to the idea of social justice presupposes that we have a "feeling of injustice about the distribution of material goods in a society of free men" (*LLL,* 2:69)—and hence we think of issuing "complaints about the outcome of the market": but in the functioning of the market, "*who* has been unjust?" It is clear that, from the viewpoint of a theory of the market as *spontaneous order,* this question has no answer: the need for social justice is thus imputed to.an absurd divinization of society, its transformation into a mysterious authority to which are addressed complaints and claims when it does not respond to the hopes it has raised—while in reality these disappointments form part of the wealth-creating process that is beneficial to all. Since "there is no individual and no cooperating group of people against which the sufferer would have a just complaint," having the state intervene to reduce these disappointments would be to commit both an error and a fault:

—An error, for every correction in the market's spontaneous order is said to create disorder in this "game of catallaxy" that "leads to an increase in the stream of goods": to correct here is to pervert the game, to change its rules, and to make it unplayable.

—A fault, for Hayek sees this game as also leading to an increase in "the chances of *all* participants to satisfy their needs." Declaring, for the sake of justice, an intervention necessary in favor of this or that *particular* group of individuals, the interest of certain ones is privileged over the chances of all—an obviously "reprehensible" step, if only morally: "a government aiming to secure for its citizens equal material positions . . . would have to treat them very unequally" (*LLL,* 2:82), whereas the only rules that a government worthy of a free people should get respected would be those favoring the catallactic functioning of a market that increased the chances of all. In short, inequality of conditions is part of the "cosmos of the market" whose internal purpose is an overall improvement of conditions and whose functioning favors "the chances of anyone selected at random" (*LLL,* 2:129–30) by fostering a society "in which the chances of anyone selected at random are likely to be as great as possible" (*LLL,* 2:132); in other words, inequality of conditions is part of a process that increases the equality of chances.

This attack on the paradoxically inegalitarian nature of the notion of social justice makes it possible to get an exact appreciation of Hayek's conceptions and to avoid the tempting confusions we just indicated: contrary to other deconstructions of modern political philosophy (we are thinking, as we have said, of Leo Strauss in particular) and despite a terminological apparatus alluding to Greek thought, Hayek's procedure does not represent an "antimodern" reaction of returning to the Platonic or Aristotelian conception of natural right. *Law, Legislation and Liberty* in fact criticizes both Plato and Hobbes for being already constructivist, and we can easily see why natural right cannot serve as a reference here: like every modern, Hayek is and remains a defender of the de jure equality of all men, each having de jure equality in the market to better his condition, that is, to increase his chances of satisfying his needs; therefore, this rules out opposing the tradition of modern natural right—even if the tradition is criticized for confusing natural law and the law of reason (natural right and subjective right) (*LLL,* 2:59ff)—an ancient natural right that we have seen is by definition *inegalitarian.* What's more, Hayek, unlike Strauss or Villey, does not make a contrast between the transcendence of some standard and the degeneration of modern natural right into juridical positivism (the height of constructivism) (*LLL,* 2:44ff), for here, the natural laws that are merely made explicit by the law are the laws of the market, and hence immanent in the market and its development (they are *organic* and *process* laws, laws of structuring and evolution). Therefore, we easily see that many criticisms made of Hayek do not apply, especially when his work is purely and simply denounced as "the gospel of inequality":[15] for though Hayek is assuredly a traditionalistic thinker, his political and legal ideas cannot be called antimodern (since they are inspired by the deeply modern recognition of the de jure equality of men), reactionary (since it is not a matter of returning, against the moderns and the declarations of formal rights, to an inegalitarian conception of right), or even conservative (since there is no question of petrifying established social conceptions, but that the preservation of the order of the market is supposed to create equal chances for all of improving their conditions). In this sense, it may not be as easy as one might think to meet Hayek's challenge to the socialist inclusion of entitlements in human rights. The movement begun by Tocqueville, and intensified more provocatively by Guizot, seems here to reach its end term: Hayek's radical liberalism totally dissociates permissions from entitlements in a condemnation seemingly without appeal of the idea of social justice, which is held to be incompatible with the defense of permissions. In this hyperbolic form, the liberal version of the discourse of human rights seems to attain a coherence that can stand up to moral indignation.

The most recent criticisms of Hayek's theses have too often been made from a simple ethical viewpoint that is in this case inappropriate. One means above all to resist the condemnation of the notion of social justice: "A society that refused to help the weak, to reduce inequalities, to foster brotherhood would not deserve to be defended and indeed would not be," for "the defense of right presupposes a wide allegiance, itself based on the belief in justice." [16] While perfectly understandable, this objection runs into three difficulties:

(*a*) First, to resist effectively the condemnation of the notion of social justice, it would have to be shown that, contrary to what Hayek maintains, this notion has a meaning; in other words, either it would have to be shown that entitlements are indeed rights, and therefore resist Hayek's argument that denouncing the injustice of some particular effect of competition naïvely assumes that this effect is to be ascribed to the responsibility of some agent; or, if we grant that entitlements are not rights, they would have to be given another status, making it possible to keep a meaning for the need for social justice: as long as we do not take this difficulty into account and do not ground the two solutions mentioned in reason, it seems hard to criticize Hayek's argument in the name of a notion (social justice) whose meaningfulness he disputes.

(*b*) In addition, it is tricky to criticize *Law, Legislation and Liberty* for defending inequalities when, as we said, Hayek defends the market precisely to the extent that its functioning seems to him beneficial for all—then condemning the redistributive policies in the name of the principle of equality before the law, the basis of the whole modern conception of right.

(*c*) It is not even easy to argue against Hayek, as did Raymond Aron in 1965, concerning the impossibility (in the interest of an effective defense of formal rights) of eliminating any assumption of responsibility for material claims. Hayek's *Toward Liberty* stresses that in giving no consideration to material needs, the theme of formal freedoms is weakened by having nothing with which to oppose the Marxist attack on them as simple tools of inequality; today, in *Law, Legislation and Liberty,* Hayek seems to answer this objection directly by judging that "there is no reason why in a free society the government should not assure to all protection against severe deprivation in the form of an assured minimum income, or a floor below which nobody need descend" (*LLL,* 2:87). Hayek himself says that it must be "a clear moral duty for all, in the organized community, to assist . . . those who cannot help themselves," and in any case no one can claim that this struggle "against extreme misfortune" would be contrary to "the interest of all." Thus we cannot without precautions claim that Hayek defends a society that "refuses to help the weak." That is why the ethical criticism clearly misfires.

Having said this, while Hayek undeniably takes the need for a minimum of resources into consideration, this taking into consideration creates problems concerning its very possibility within his conception of the social. The *problem of fact* does not arise—Hayek clearly recognizes the need for a system of guarantees against a "severe deprivation." On the other hand, the *problem of right* does arise: is this recognition possible and coherent in the context of such a radical liberalism? This problem is clear in the passage just quoted: because even a minimal politics of redistribution would amount to intervening in the order of the market and thus disrupting the functioning "favorable to all" (egalitarian), Hayek must immediately spell out "that such a uniform income [must be] provided *outside the market* to all those who, for any reason, are unable to earn in the market an adequate maintenance"; in this case and this case only, "this need not lead to a restriction of freedom, or conflict with the Rule of Law," hence nothing that can put the market mechanism "out of the game." We obviously cannot wonder about the meaning of this benefit "out of the market." Negatively, this clearly rules out any system of allocation fixed by authority, or any device by which this authority would allocate to certain individuals with various goods at lower prices than those resulting from the law of the market: this solution would irremediably distort the "game of catallaxy" and work against the principle of an equal right for all. But positively? An article by Nathan Glazer[17] suggests that, in contemporary societies in which the poor represent only a limited fraction of the population (10–20 percent), protection against "severe deprivation" does not come within the domain of public services, thus of the welfare state, but of private assistance, "voluntary help," "a nonpublic action"—in short, charity or the privatization of the problem of entitlements! Is this the solution Hayek is thinking of? Truth to tell, this question is impossible to answer, and it is surely not without significance that the question remains undecidable here. For here we reach a limit of the theoretical model on which Hayek's whole construction rests: if the self-development of the market is "beneficial to all," any political initiative to correct the effects of this self-development is de jure impossible to legitimate; if, faced with difficulties, not just moral ones (see Aron's 1965 objection) to which a total rejection of the problem of social justice would be exposed, we are forced to grant a minimal assumption of responsibility for the needs embodied in the notion of entitlements, it then remains to refer the solution to individual initiatives, thus to charity. The theme of charity, present in Tocqueville's writing on the right to work and accentuated by Guizot in *Democracy in France,* thus remains the last word of the liberal tradition, even when it wishes to be "neoliberal," about the problem of entitlements: the liberal solution to the problem is decidedly *nonpolitical.*

It would be easy to stress what is haphazard or derisory about such a solution on a practical level. It seems to us more fruitful to show how this difficulty, whose root is *theoretical,* leads us to the real limits of Hayek's challenge or, more globally, to the real difficulties with a liberal model, of which Hayek's version magnifies certain possibilities owing to its hyperbolic character. The more serious difficulties encountered by Hayek's attempt are of a theoretical kind, and lie in the inability of this fierce opponent of Marxism truly to avoid an *intellectual structure* singularly close to the one his own thinking sets up as an antitype. On two points, Hayek's hyperliberalism proves unable to offer a true theoretical alternative to the socialism of Marxist origin.

(1) Against constructivism, Hayek appeals to an evolutionism that entrusts the improvement of conditions to the self-development of the market. This evolutionism is, however, a historicism: market order results from a spontaneous and not a conscious process (it is the result of competition), and, similarly, the rules and institutions that the government gets respected to preserve the "game of catallaxy" are described as products of *history*—products of "the natural selection of the social institutions and rules of conduct" (the rules prove to give "the most vigor" to the group). Thus, both the market order and the rules making possible its creation and functioning are *historical*—and it is not hard to understand why it *must* be this way to Hayek's way of thinking: only such a historicism, which makes the socioeconomic order and its rules necessarily the product of a process immanent in history, allows for the elimination in principle of voluntarism and the resolute condemnation of any constructivist conception of organization. One can then state the structure or, if you will, the theoretical infrastructure of Hayek's hyperliberalism: clearly, in a paradox that is merely apparent, we see here the structure of "the cunning of reason" whose survival we have already noted in Marxist historicism. One could pick out many significant formulations of this in Hayek's writings: "In the Great Society we all in fact

contribute not only to the satisfaction of needs of which we do not know, but sometimes even to the achievement of ends of which we would disapprove if we knew about them" (*LLL*, 2:109–10); "in the catallaxy men, while following their own interests, whether wholly egotistical or highly altruistic, will further the aims of many others, most of whom they will never know" (*LLL*, 2:110). May we be allowed not to demonstrate once again that this structure is the very one of historicism? Hayek's hyperliberalism is a hyperrationalism, presup-posing, like Hegel's, that "in history everything unfolds rationally" and that even the seemingly most unreasonable initiatives have something of the nature of self-fulfillment of a rationality (here that of the market) in constant evolution. Hayek even explicitly indicates that the development of the market is in this sense an "impersonal process," in which "there is no subject" (*LLL*, 2:78): the theoretical convergence of Hayek's evolutionism and the Hegelian-Marxist his-toricism of the "process without subject" thus goes into the lexicon! From such a convergence one could then find a clearer confirmation of Hayek's rallying to the thesis of the *relativism of values* (*LLL*, 2:26–27): "all the moral (and juridical) rules serve an existing concrete order" and "hence there can be no absolute system of morality in-dependent of the kind of social order in which a person finds himself living"—which Hayek feels the need to illustrate by the dubious but significant example that for him, "it would be clearly morally bad to revive an elderly and already unconscious Eskimo" whom his people, at the time of their winter migration and following their eth-ical principles, had left behind and exposed to certain death! Beyond what seems ridiculous or scandalous in this example, we can easily see the deeply *antijuridical* implications of this relativism of values, the ritual companion (fellow traveler?) of historicism: for how, from this perspective, to make permissions some sort of sacred values, respect for which should furnish the government with its categorical imperative? Here we come upon the supreme paradox of the gulf between permissions and entitlements that has not ceased to yawn in the liberal tradition: by trying to preserve permissions from the perverse effects of voluntarism and interventionism most often in-duced by the theme of entitlements made on the state, liberalism ends up trusting everything to history (here the self-development of the market)—thus re-creating a representation (the historicist one) of this very history that takes away all real meaning and impact from the proclamation of permissions themselves. One is thus led from the criticism of social justice to the historicist dissolution of permissions. This singular movement is confirmed by a second dimension of Hayek's thought, as it too, with its historicism, is curiously reminiscent of its Marxist opponent.

(2) What's more, Hayek's evolutionism is an economism, and here too the shadow of Marxism, the dead God, definitely continues to lengthen. Since the market order enables it to harmonize and make compatible the divergent plans of individuals, the social is created by the economic ("the only ties which hold the whole of a Great Society together are purely economic, more precisely catallactic"[*LLL,* 2:112]), and that in addition gives rise to politics (the rules and institutions that politics gets respected) as the condition of possibility of a well-functioning market. This setting up of the economy as "the final authority" of the social order then is to be quite naturally expressed in terms strikingly reminiscent of the famous 1890 letter to Bloch in which Engels described how in the social "There is an interaction of all these elements in which, amid all the endless host of accidents (that is, of things and events whose inner interconnection is so remote or so impossible of proof that we can regard it as nonexistent, as negligible), the economic movement finally asserts itself as necessary." [18] Hayek writes: "It is of course true that within the overall framework of the Great Society there exist numerous networks of other relations that are in no sense economic. But this does not alter the fact that it is the market order which makes peaceful reconciliation of the divergent purposes possible—and possible by a process which redounds to the benefit of all" (*LLL,* 2:112). Thus it is the economic process (the market) that creates the social nexus and that determines which of the alleged natural rights is actualizable— politics then being merely a tool for this actualization that in the final instance it does not determine. Hayek's evolutionism is a historicism and an economism: it is a theory of the cunning of economic reason—the theoretical structure constitutive of Marxism and its negation of right here being put in the service of what consequently appeared less the antithesis of Marxism than its fraternal enemy.

It would be easy to spot the difficulties to which Hayek is then exposed, and they are present in every theory of the cunning of reason: if the self-deployment of a process without a subject actualizes what is "favorable to all," how can we criticize the existence of any institutional form whatever? If an institutional form has survived the process of the natural selection of institutions, isn't that a proof that it has social efficacy? [19] In this case, how can Hayek criticize the state institutions of contemporary societies? The contradiction is clear: it is traditionally the lot of a historicist hyperrationalism never to manage to follow its own implications to the end—if only in that the (finite) subject expressing these theses (who defines evolution as a process without a subject) would have to efface itself, to die to itself to the point of relinquishing all critical perspective (any value judgment) with regard to any moment in a process whose necessity it would be its role simply to record. We shall not return here to the insuperable aporias of this philosophy of history.[20] The point here is to see that it prevents the reference to human rights (if only permissions) from having any critical function whatever: in this sense, the discourse of human rights, purged of the theme of entitlements and reduced to the proclamation of permissions, comes to lose, in this context, both *its meaning* (expressing *atemporal* rights of man as such, passing for *universals*) and its *function* (to contrast between the positivity of historically variable institutions and the norms for the sake of which these institutions can be criticized, to contrast the "ought" or ideal and the "is" or the real). So much that where Marxist socialism, overprivileging entitlements, ended up devalorizing permissions, the neoliberalism that is claimed to oppose it, manages the feat of *both* reducing entitlements to a "mirage" and depriving permissions of what might lend their proclamation some genuine impact.

It will be said that in the liberal tradition Hayek represents a dubious extremism and that conclusions based on such an example are overstated. It remains true, however, that the seductiveness of Hayek's thinking is due precisely to its hyperbolic character and that, to dismiss what is hyperliberal in Hayek, the neoliberalism that is to provide the alternative solution and the remedy for all ills after the collapse of socialist illusions, does not seem to be "*neo*liberalism" only in name; we have sufficiently stressed in our introduction not to have to repeat them here the political difficulties of withdrawing to a more classical liberalism. We would merely add that to our minds the historicism attacked in Hayek represents a simple expansion of a possibility in the liberal thought in Constant and Tocqueville. As Philippe Raynaud has shown,[21] Constant's criticism of political voluntarism tends to rely on the idea of society as a "self-regulated system," society unifying itself without external intervention, through the convergence of individual wills: "Lost in the crowd, the individual never notices the influence he exerts. Never does his will leave its mark on the whole; nothing places his cooperation conclusively before his own eyes."[22] The schema of the cunning of reason is already present here. Certainly, Constant is not fully and exclusively wedded to this schema, since, because he never fully considered the real and the rational as identical,[23] he can keep a reference to human rights as norms defining an "ought." It is a matter of interpretation whether this incompletion is a strength or a weakness (meaning inconsequentiality), but it is still true that in Constant, the liberal criticism of the political theories that ground social unity on the voluntarist intervention of a political power is possible only through "the adoption, in an elementary form, of a perspective that was to find its completed form in Hegel's theory of the cunning of reason"[24] and that, in the subsequent history of liberalism, animates the main criticisms of the welfare state in Hayek's evolutionism.[25] Thus, for someone who today wants to endorse the liberal tradition, it is not so easy to dismiss the alleged excesses to which Hayek supposedly gives himself over: Hayek's hyperliberalism represents a historicist and economist tendency of the most classical liberalism, and consequently, if this path be followed, it is not certain that the discourse of human rights can escape a new and more insidious dismissal.

CHAPTER FIVE

From Human Rights to the
Republican Idea

The analysis of the problems uncovered in the discourse of human rights—starting with the privilege granted entitlements and an exclusive valorization of permissions—leads us to look for the conditions for synthesizing these two types of rights that the history of the declarations of human rights and their interpretations have made to seem antinomial. With greater or lesser felicity, this synthesis has been explicitly attempted by two traditions: that of social democracy and that of republicanism. Examining the current of democratic socialism from this viewpoint, we pay particular attention to its French representatives, though in many ways the German contributions, particularly Eduard Bernstein's, have a greater claim on our sympathies (if only through the clearer philosophical relations with Kantianism); at least three reasons prompt us to begin with the socialism of Jean Jaurès: (1) because the Revolution of 1848 seemed to have occasioned the real debate between liberals and socialists about the interpretation of human rights, the French tradition formed the privileged area for inquiring about the position taken by another socialism at the core of this debate; (2) as we shall see, democratic socialism in France contains significant ambiguities—and particularly interesting ones for our purpose—difficulties in the socialist tradition's escaping its past: the limits of this first attempt at synthesis can thus be clearly brought to light; (3) while there are fewer ambiguities in Bernstein, it is to the precise extent that, with Jaurès, fidelity to the socialist tradition here does not as clearly overshadow the real nature of the synthesis, that is, the republican project.

1. Jaurès's Democratic Socialism: The Break with Marxism

In the important 1901 article in which he critically analyzed Marx and Engels's *Communist Manifesto,*[1] Jaurès declares in plain language that "Marx's decisive merit, the only one which fully withstands the tests of critique and the deep wounds of time, is the fact of having brought together and made one the socialist idea and the workers' movement." As for the rest, which we recognize is not negligible, Marx's method, still a captive of the violent activism of Auguste Blanqui and François Noël Babeuf, is "in its entirety and whichever way one looks at it . . . out of date." In the later part of the text, which is in many ways reminiscent of Bernstein's revisionist criticism, Jaurès shows how the Marxist conception of the revolution, like its implied vision of democracy and the so-called formal rights, corresponds not only to a bygone stage of the development of the proletariat, but is very much mistaken in its very principle.

The themes of French democratic socialism's break with Marxism are in the main well known.[2] We merely recall two elements that imply a rejection of historicism and hence give us a better grasp of Jaurès's attitude toward the question of human rights: the conception of the revolution and the theory of the state.

The concern of democratic socialism to break with a practice of politics that somehow implies the suspension, even temporary, of legality or, if you will, the principle of formal democracy is best expressed in Jaurès's criticism of the Marx's Blanquism—a theme he also shares with Bernstein.[3] Two theses stated in his *Question of Method* warrant our attention here:

(1) The dictatorship of the proletariat, as Marx and Engels conceived of it, must drive the proletariat only to barbarism and eventually to failure. When they assert that the proletariat "conquers democracy" through force, it would be more exact to say, according to their theory, "that it in fact suspends it, since for the will of a majority of freely consulted citizens it substitutes the dictatorial will of one class." This practice would be doubly erroneous. On the one hand, the resort to violence presupposes a weak and minority proletariat that must, according to the Babouvist and Blanquist tactics, benefit from a bourgeois revolution that it deflects to its own advantage. This time is past, and "it is openly, on the field of democratic legality and the universal vote that the socialist proletariat prepares, extends, organizes the revolution." On the other hand, "the proletarian revolution itself originating in a vast movement toward democracy," it cannot turn against it. "A class issued from democracy which, instead of rallying to the law of the majority, would prolong its dictatorship past the first days of the revolution, would soon become nothing more than a troop, camping on the territory and abusing of the country's resources."

(2) So it must be affirmed that, far from needing to use and abuse force, the proletariat today has "through democracy and universal suffrage, an infinitely expandable legal force. It is not reduced to being the adventurous and violent parasite of bourgeois revolutions. It methodically prepares or, better, methodically begins its own revolution through the gradual and legal conquest of the power of production and the power of the state."

Thus we find that Marx and Engels's error in the *Manifesto* at two levels:

—First, the dialectical conception of history itself needs to be revised: this conception suggests a politics of the worst, connected with the idea that the revolution can break out only when the poverty and suffering of the proletariat have reached their height. It puts "on the scales a depressive force which acts immediately"—the proletarization and pauperism that accentuate suffering—"and a force of organization and resistance which above all seems to prepare the future"—the hostile reaction of the proletariat in the face of its increasing poverty—while in fact the working class is constantly stronger, more cultivated, and less poor. So "Marx was mistaken": "it is not from absolute destitution that absolute liberation could come."

—Next, Marx and Engels misjudged capitalism's ability to accept compromises with the proletariat. Thus Engels "adopted an analysis of the inflexibility of the capitalist system, of its powerlessness to adapt itself to the most minor reform, which is so rigid and strict, that he makes the most serious and decisive mistakes in his interpretation of social movements ... everywhere he saw incompatibilities, impossibilities, unsolvable contradictions which could be resolved only by revolution," which leads him to predict a catastrophe in England as imminent as it is bloody, in the course of which "the poor will cut rich men's throats and burn their castles," which effectively constitutes a "strange view of this country of England, always so talented when it comes to evolutions and compromises"!

Thus the Socialist party—this is Jaurès's conclusion, who here again, as in his whole argumentation, is closest to Bernstein—must become one with "the nation, through its definitive acceptance of democracy and legality." We can thus easily understand that on Jaurès's death, Lenin, who was asked to write an article on his work, answered: "To write ill of him today would be a nuisance, but I see nothing good to write. The thing to do is simply to keep quiet."

Formulated for the most part in two speeches, "Address to Youth" and the "Toulouse Address,"[4] as well as in *Democracy and Military*

Service, Jaurès's theory of the state continues this break with Marxism and, more generally, all the historicist examples of the suspension of democratic principles for the sake of the "final goal." As for the state, Jaurès is opposed to the Marxist vulgate on three main points:

(1) First, Jaurès rejects what could be called the Manicheanism of the class struggle. Against the idea that in history only one of the classes in conflict could be the bearer of a positive and universal message, he emphasizes that "the two antagonistic classes have a mutual interest in seeing to it that each class possess the highest moral and intellectual force," since "the conflict which divides them and inflames them" must finally be resolved not by a victory of one over the other, but by a "higher solidarity." Thus political pluralism is grounded in the social structure itself.

(2) It is therefore clear that the state cannot long be thought the tool of the dominant class, but must, which is quite different, appear the place where class antagonism is expressed: "the state is not the expression of one class; it expresses the relationship between classes," writes Jaurès, and in the *Democracy and Military Service* he argues against Marx that "there has never been a state which has purely and simply been a class-bound state"—such that even the bourgeois state already expresses the demands of the working class and in proportion to the degree of consciousness and organization the class has reached.[5]

(3) The role of the state is thus essentially one of arbitration, the values of formal or parliamentary democracy thus imposing themselves equally on the two classes: "the proletariat cannot refuse this sovereign arbitration of democracy, for democracy is the context within which the classes maneuver." Jaurès's formulation is significant here: the expressions "context" and "arbitration" refer to the idea that, contrary to Marxism, the democratic state is a neutral and universal element, higher than the class struggle and hence higher than history. Thus, Jaurès sees the legal and political sphere as autonomous from history.

On the purely philosophical level, it would be easy to show how "in the final analysis" this break with Marxism is rooted in a completely explicit "idealist prejudgment" according to which "humanity, from its very beginnings, possesses, so to speak, an obscure idea, a first premonition of its destiny, of its development."[6] Thus the economic infrastructure does not determine human thought according to a dialectical scheme that would reduce it to the status of pure reflection, but "before the experience of history, before the constitution of such and such economic systems, humanity carries within itself a previous idea of justice and law . . . [and] when humanity goes into action, it is not due to the mechanical, automatic transformation of modes of production, but under the obscurely or clearly felt influence of this ideal." [7] With these lines Jaurès expressly situates himself in a tradition of thought going back to Kant and Fichte, as is clearly shown by his interesting thesis about the origins of German socialism. [8]

Jaurès's attitude toward the 1789 Declaration of the Rights of Man was quite different from Marx's. His discussion of it in *Histoire socialiste de la Révolution française* [9] even curiously foreshadows the criticism of Marx that we saw in Claude Lefort [10]—with Jaurès attempting with surprising perspicacity to detect the universal significance behind the "bourgeois" version of human rights, and hence their validity for the proletariat: "In its struggle against the Most High, the revolutionary bourgeoisie had to lift itself up to humanity, at the risk of superseding its own laws and discerning a new law far away. It is this class intrepidness, this boldness in forging sovereign weapons— even if history should one day turn them against the conqueror— which makes the greatness of the revolutionary bourgeoisie. In this way among others the work of the Revolution was universal for an entire period of history." Thus, "the Declaration of the Rights of Man . . . will become the formula for the proletarian revolution."

2. The Ambiguities of Democratic Socialism in France

Incorporating values that are liberal, more reformist than revolutionary, and profoundly humanistic—everything must, it seems, lead French democratic socialism in Jaurès's tradition to "dare to seem what it was" and to produce a conversion similar to what its German cousin had known under the influence of Eduard Bernstein. And yet at least until recently, the socialist tradition in France surely has been marked by serious ambiguities in its attitude toward human rights and, more generally, the values of formal democracy.

Jaurès's anti-Marxist stands were frequently obscured by rhetorical and political needs, as he himself almost explicitly recognizes in a text that deserves to be quoted because it sheds so much (good-humored) light on his method. In *Question of Method,* after severely criticizing the Marxist thesis of the revolution as an inevitable reaction to pauperization, Jaurès writes:

Here is indeed Marx and Engels's way of thinking at this time. I am of course aware that nowadays some seek to veil the brutality of these texts. I know that subtle Marxist interpreters are saying that Marx and Engels meant to speak of a "relative" pauperization. Thus, when theologians wish to reconcile the biblical texts with scientifically verified reality, they say that in the book of Genesis the word "day" indicates a geological period of many million years. I do not contradict in the least. These are matters of elegance and of exegetical indulgence which allow for a painless transition from long-held dogma to better known truth. And since "revolutionary" spirits need such careful handling, who would dream of thwarting them?

A concession humorous in its tone, certainly, but nevertheless raises a question that, because it crops up throughout the history of French socialism, ends up less humorous: wasn't Jaurès a great theologian as well, for example, when he went against all self-evidence and took the side of the orthodox German Marxist Karl Kautsky against the revisionist Bernstein by asserting in his essay on Bernstein that "in the controversy that arose between Bernstein and Kautsky about the principles and method of socialism, I stand, on the whole, with Kautsky."[11]

Here we give only one piece of evidence, to our eyes largely and sufficiently significant, of these ambiguities with regard to permissions in French socialism. One fundamental aspect of Jaurès's criticism of "Blanquism," revolutionary activism, lies in the (pre-anti-Leninist) idea that for the revolution not to be violent, it must be preceded by a slow process of maturation. This is the whole problem of the relation between education and revolution. For Jaurès, educating the masses must not take place *after* the revolution, but *before* it, or else it will inevitably founder in the terrorism in which the conditions of formal democracy are indefinitely suspended. In democratic socialism, the revolution thus appears as the end of a process leading to socialism, and not as a starting point that has to come after an in-principle transitional (and in reality long-lasting) dictatorship. Also in this sense Léon Blum, in the famous speech at Tours, some aspects of which we mentioned in our introduction, also condemns as "Blanquist" "the tactics of the unconscious masses dragged unwittingly by their avant-garde." And yet, at the Congress of Amsterdam of 1905, Jaurès unhesitatingly delivered a veritable indictment of the German social democrats to whom he declared: "The two essential forces, the two essential means of action of the proletariat, still escape you: you have neither revolutionary action, nor parliamentary action"—thus making equal these two principles that he everywhere else had not only distinguished between, but carefully organized into a hierarchy, and criticizing the German proletariat for receiving universal suffrage "from on high" instead of winning it through revolutionary action. And in his preface to the French translation of Kautsky's *Socialism and Parliamentarism,* he still takes Kautsky's side, for Kautsky had seen that "it is the organized proletariat, with the force of class, that must undo *all* the knots"! In a fairly similar way, but with much more glaring contradictions, Léon Blum declared at the Congress of Tours: "Reformism, or more precisely, revisionism, no longer exists . . . I know only one socialism, a revolutionary socialism." Let us confess that in reading these lines, one thinks one is dreaming—all the more so as Blum adds, explicitly against German reformism, that the term revolution "means, for traditional French socialism, the transformation from an economic regime based on private property to a regime based on collective or common property." In short, we are here sent back from reform to revolution in such a contradictory way that it could not *avoid* creating a problem. Thus, at the Socialist Congress of 1926, Blum proposed the now-famous distinction between the conquest and the exercise of power. Regarding the conquest of power, Blum says no socialist can be required to be fully legalistic and revolutionary action can never be ruled out. In the exercise of power, however, it is incumbent to conform strictly to the democratic laws in force, which Blum summarizes as follows: "Although I am not a legalist as regards the conquest of power, I am a legalist as regards the exercise of power."

Hence a constant ambiguity in the French socialist tradition, which is *in fact* legalistic not only in the exercise of power, but also quite obviously in its conquest, although *in theory* it continues to indulge in laughably revolutionary discourse and condemns that socialism never to dare to appear what it is. Hence, too, it seems to us, the equivocalness of the socialist attitude toward what in the Socialist party was never called anything but Bolshevism. Despite insuperable divergences, Blum constantly stressed—we now better understand why—"the communality of doctrinal ends" that unites the French Socialist party with Bolshevism or, to repeat another of its slogans, "their identity of final goals," since in both cases "property is transformed by means of the class action of the proletariat." What's more, while Jaurès in the *Discours à la jeunesse,* for example, explicitly condemned every idea of a "even a brief dictatorship," Blum contested in the Tours speech only the Bolshevist *interpretation* of this dictatorship, but not the dictatorship itself: "Dictatorship of a party, yes, dictatorship of a class, yes, dictatorship of some known or unknown individuals, no"—which, the reader will concede, is all the same to display a truly *minimal* sensitivity to the question of dictatorship and the ensuing suspension of freedom rights!

We are forced to admit that French democratic socialism, especially beginning with Blum, has had little success becoming doctrinally clear about the problem of the status of permissions (even when we grant that it does not *in fact* think of suspending them even temporarily). Are the reasons for this murkiness purely strategic or more deeply theoretical? That is a hard question, one that surely deserves a more detailed examination.[12] The fact remains that from this viewpoint the republican tradition, with which democratic socialism is pleased to identify itself, seems to have become somewhat obscure and to have given precedence to equivocations of tactics and ideology. Hence, if, as Blum himself affirmed,[13] Jaurès's socialism is a "deepening of the idea of a republic," "a sort of deduction of the republican principles,"[14] it must be agreed that this deepening has not always made possible a genuine reconciliation of permissions and entitlements, the needs for entitlements here continuing to threaten permissions with a suspension that Jaurès's heirs seem to be radically unable to rule out. Thus it may behoove us to return from this putative "deepening," to "the republican idea" itself, since, at the very least, the republican tradition has always made the sovereignty and even the sanctity of the law one of its inviolable principles.

3. The Republican Idea

It is important to locate this "republicanism"—which may represent the truth of Jaurès's thought when it can resist the demands and reflexes of militant practice—in a vast doctrinal movement featuring both an accentuated reference to the content of the Declarations of the Rights of Man and the search for an original position that is not simply *liberal* yet without a claim to be *socialist*. In his remarkable *L'Idée républicaine en France*,[15] Claude Nicolet has shown how a "republican reason" was formed, particularly through the experience and the reversals of 1848 (*IR*, 137ff.). This reason was a complex mixture of ideas and sentiments that it would be wrong to believe reducible to the political practice of those compromises, as complicated as they were fragile, that marked the history of the French Third Republic. On at least two points the inspiration of the chief republican doctrinarians of the nineteenth century (from Alphonse de Lamartine to Jules Ferry and Léon Gambetta, and including the less well-known but essential contributions of J. Barni, Etienne Vacherot, and Jules Simon) deserves our attention here.

(1) "Republicanism" is first and foremost the desire to realize and enrich the "heritage of human rights" (*IR,* 346). The writers of the Constitution of 1848 showed this intention in article 3 of the preamble by proclaiming that the republic "recognizes rights and duties prior to and superior to positive laws." One constant feature of republican thought is to refer to the notion of natural right, irreducible to positive right that is actualized in history: against a whole *historicist* tradition within which socialism, as we have seen, came to transmit the ancestral theses of monarchical absolutism,[16] the republicans maintain, in the famous words of Rabaud Saint-Etienne, that "our history is not our code"—in other words, a rule gets its legitimacy not from its inscription in history but only from its conformity to the ahistorical requirements of reason. In this regard it is significant to recall that in 1844 Alexandre Ledru-Rollin, whose role and importance in the history of the Republican party are well known, wrote one of the first criticisms of the historical school of law that in Germany, through the impetus of Friedrich von Savigny, meant to make the science of law simply a branch of history: thus treating *De l'influence de l'école française sur le droit au XIXe siècle,* Ledru-Rollin accuses the historical school of leading to a fatalistic conception of law, and in doing this, of "denying politics"[17]—moreover adding, and here again the remark is not without impact or, in advance, devoid of lucidity—that the socialists do the same when they privilege the "satisfaction of material needs" over strictly political reforms. That this juridical antihistoricism has remained, beyond influences and developments,[18] the common basis of republicanism is a fact whose conditions of intellectual possibility we shall have to determine, but one that in any case already explains both the unshakeable attachment of the republicans to the *atemporal* content of the declarations and their resistance to the blandishments of socialist doctrines that are otherwise less distrustful about history.

(2) Though the intellectual configuration defining republicanism made possible the antihistoricist affirmation of the untranscendable value of the Declarations of the Rights of Man and thus sanctioned a consequent discourse on human rights, fully assuming the normative legal impact of these declarations, we must still spell out how the republican tradition interpreted this content. For the repub-

licans, what is the sphere of legal values that seems irreducible to the conditions of their emergence? The least that can be said about the liberals' and socialists' interpretations is that they were unlikely (we have seen why) for winning minds to the content of the declarations: sometimes playing permissions against possible entitlements, sometimes those entitlements against the merely formal character of permissions, liberals and socialists have made human rights primarily an axis of division. In this regard also, the republican position shows its originality. Certainly, for the republicans the declarations of reference were the ones accompanying the Constitutions of 1793 and the Year III, that is, texts that, as we noted in our introduction, more than the Declaration of 1789, repeated in the preamble of the Constitution of 1791—put the consideration of the "common happiness" "goal of society" next to freedom rights. This privileging the texts of 1793 is already enough to distinguish the republican discourse of human rights from liberal discourse—insofar as, for example, Constant anticipated the condemnation of entitlements in the subsequent history of liberalism by saying to the authors of the *montagnarde* Constitution: "Let authority be confined to being just: we shall assume the responsibility for being happy." [19] And yet this antiliberal recognition of the "common happiness" as "a goal of society" never impelled the republicans to adopt the socialist theme of entitlements. Even when in 1834 the *Revue républicaine* contrasted a right higher than the individual to the liberals' "absolute individual right," the writer of the article[20] stated that this "social right" in fact refers to a duty of solidarity with the community that merely makes the very idea of "fraternity" explicit: adding to individual rights a social right by which the nation not only protects individual freedoms, but also ensures the subsistence of its most destitute components, the republican doctrine thus went little further than what was already recognized in article 21 of the declaration joined to the *montagnarde* Constitution ("Public assistance is a sacred debt. Society owes the unfortunate citizens a subsistence").[21] How then can we reconcile the antiliberal recognition of the "common happiness as a goal of society" with this refusal to follow the socialists in their enrollment of entitlements among the rights of man? Here is exactly where republican discourse about human rights finds its specificity: genuine human rights are the rights of the citizen as political rights to participate in power, essentially through universal suffrage—*participation* rights that, on the one hand, presuppose permissions, and, on the other hand, through their very exercise, guarantee the assumption of responsibility for the needs for solidarity or fraternity. Let us briefly explain this twofold articulation:

(*a*) There is a clear link between participation rights and permissions: for republicans, the best guarantee of permissions seems to lie in the citizens' authentic participation in sovereignty through universal suffrage; it is clear that the truly democratic exercise of universal suffrage presupposes respect for basic freedoms (of opinion, of the press, of assembly, and so on) without which the expression of the people's will would be impossible or inevitably distorted. This faith in universal suffrage, constant in the republican tradition, was certainly shaken when in December of 1848 the ballot boxes decreed Louis-Napoléon to be elected president of the republic. Nevertheless, it is still true that the Republican party always considered universal suffrage "the only possible basis for our political organization," [22] but limited itself to enriching the dogma of universal suffrage by bringing out the theme of the necessary *education* of the citizens as, in Gambetta's formula, "the education of universal suffrage": the democratic exercise of universal suffrage thus presupposes not only the fundamental freedoms, but also the equality of the right to education. Hence the educational policies of the Third Republic: democracy (the authentic exercise of universal suffrage) exists only through the school, in other words, "democracy is demopedy."

(*b*) Less obvious is the articulation between the exercise of participation rights and the assumption of responsibility for the needs for solidarity. We know the Marxist (or Proudhonian) criticism of the right to vote as a mere formal right not implying any satisfaction of the real rights of individuals. In fact, here again it is one of Gambetta's formulas, repeated in several speeches between 1872 and 1878, that best expresses the republican conviction: the republic, that is, primarily the practice of universal suffrage, is "a form that entails the content." The republic, whose law is necessarily the law of number (for the majority of the people, through their representatives, makes the law), cannot survive without ensuring decent living conditions for the most populous classes. Where universal suffrage is truly free and educated, this *formal* condition of democracy concerning the *content* of governmental decisions thus inevitably involves the assumption of responsibility—perhaps partial, perhaps slow and gradual—for the needs of social solidarity. At the same time that participation rights presuppose respect for permissions, their exercise ensures the gradual actualization of what socialists consider entitlements. It is easily shown that this is the source of most of the great themes of the republican tradition: the idea of the sovereignty and sanctity of the law, expression of universal suffrage, the primacy granted politics and the question of the form of the regime (the principle of popular sovereignty implies universal suffrage, the republic is consequently the only regime consistent with the principles of 1789 and the only one able both to guarantee freedoms and to satisfy the needs for solidarity), the supremacy of the legislative and, correspondingly, the question of the separation of powers (sovereignty is in the assembly produced by universal suffrage, for any division of sovereignty threatens national unity), and so forth.

We shall not go further here in the discussion of what can henceforth be called the *republican synthesis:* that the republican idea can have a unifying value is not only a question of *fact* that could be resolved by recalling this or that period of French political history in which various groups have rallied around republican themes (see first part of *IR*); the unifying value of the republican idea is rather defined as de jure when it is granted that the principal source of a possible solution to the antinomy of permissions and entitlements, which continues to oppose the liberal and the socialist traditions, lies in the notion of participation rights. To recognize that this is the key to a solution (hence the principle of a genuine recovered consensus around the reference to human rights) is not, however, to consider that this evocation of the republican idea will magically solve all problems. The theme of participation rights poses many practical problems meaning those of concrete politics: independent of questions raised by the exercise of universal suffrage,[23] it may be asked, for example, at what levels, aside from the election of representatives to the national assembly, these participation rights can be exercised and in what forms—a problem that is easily seen to involve the problem of centralization and autonomy[24] and that has provoked many debates in the republican tradition about the status of local communities (In the final analysis is the "public weal" the national state, or are there rights inherent to participation in the life of the local community?). We set aside these various problems, which basically represent the implementation of the *idea,* and limit ourselves to examining the *theoretical* problems that might be posed by the idea itself. There is at least one that presents itself rather obviously: in defining freedom as the participation of the citizen in public life, doesn't republican reason involve an *ancient* conception of citizenship? As such, isn't it vulnerable to Benjamin Constant's criticisms contrasting the requirements of freedom in the moderns (that of a limitation of sovereignty and an autonomy of the individual in relation to the sovereign authority) to Rousseau's conception of freedom as participation in sovereignty? We see what is at stake with this problem: if the republican synthesis represents an *ancient* conception of freedom, it cannot claim to resolve the antinomy between the main political theories of modernity—except to revive the mirage of a return to the ancients, whose aporias we analyzed at the beginning of this book.

In his book, Claude Nicolet seem to grant that republican reason essentially refers to a conception of "ancient-style citizenship" (*IR,* 395ff.) and stresses that "the distant but common origin of all doctrines of this kind rests on the model of the ancient city" (*IR,* 396). His thinking even concludes with the recognition that "the republican tradition, especially when it tries to incorporate modernity, in fact more or less consciously rejects the break" between ancient freedom and modern freedom that is wholly accepted by the Anglo-Saxons" and by the French liberals—to remain indissolubly attached to the ancient model, which was just about wholly that of Rousseau. Through the Rousseauean inspiration, it is the ancient inspiration that dominated the republican tradition (*IR,* 480–81).[25] Not only, we repeat, do we think this conclusion leads to largely relativizing the currentness of the republican idea,[26] it seems to us debatable for two reasons—or, if you prefer, we think the republican idea belongs to modernity in two ways:

(*a*) First, it will surely easily be granted, one characteristic feature of political modernity is the autonomization of the political in relation to theological authority:[27] if *secularism* is one of the key words unarguably summarizing the struggle of the republicans in the nineteenth century, and if it is granted that, mythically or not, this struggle represents an attempt to free political reason from theological authority, it will be agreed that this is a first indication of the republican traditions' inscription in modernity.

(*b*) More importantly, if "the great affair of the republicans is of course Rousseau" (*IR,* 70), in that republican freedom, like Rousseau's, is defined by participating in sovereign power-wielding,[28] it must be stressed that in both Rousseau and his republican heirs these conceptions of freedom and politics "presuppose a people and a public interest as the only source of sovereignty (*IR,* 396); in chapter 2 we sufficiently indicated how the emergence of this theme of popular sovereignty was inseparable from the theoretical conditions of possibility that are constitutive of modernity and that as such are unthinkable in the ancient world, for us merely to refer the reader to these analyses: aside from the metaphors appealing to antiquity that republican orators reveled in (Gambetta unhesitatingly compared "the French republic in the modern world" to "the Athenian republic in antiquity"), the republican idea proceeds from a resolutely modern reason.

It obviously remains to spell out what this republican reason is. Aside from the philosophical eclecticism of the republican culture,[29] one observation is called for after Nicolet's learned studies: a certain *Kantian* reference insistently intervenes among those doctrinarians seeking a theoretical foundation for the idea. The influence of J. Barni, the translator of Kant and Fichte, in the Republican party is highly significant in this regard (see *IR* 302). Beginning in the Second Empire, the role taken by university professors like Jules Simon, Etienne Vacherot, Charles Renouvier, and even, later on, by Alain, confirms an impressive dominance of Kantianism in nineteenth-century republican thought. That being so, what Kantianism is involved? Nicolet has given us a fine analysis of this: as a critical rationalism, Kantianism allows republican reason to combine the assertion of rational content (particularly the values embodied in the Declarations of the Rights of Man) that is a priori understandable and hence irreducible to history, and despite everything—against an empiricism that easily gives way to skepticism and, on a practical level, to realism—to sustain the project of a politics grounded on reason without yielding to the dogmatic forms of socialist reason (*IR,* 265). We confess that this is a minimal, banal, and pedantic Kantianism. It is, true enough, the version of Kantianism that was most frequently taught in French universities, and we are unsurprised to find the traces of it here. It is not, however, forbidden us to consider this Kantian reference as an indication and an incentive to push further ahead in the analysis of the relations between critical reason and republican reason.

4. The Republic as an Idea of Reason

In the Kantian tradition there is a well-established custom and this up to its most contemporary figures:[30] that of making a careful distinction between two forms of knowledge: understanding and reason. The republican idea, insofar as it appears to be the solution of the ideal-typical antinomy between the liberal conception of human rights (the rejection of entitlements) and the Marxist conception of them (the at-least-temporary suspension of permissions), clearly needs to be thought through with the help of this distinction. For clarity of exposition, we briefly recall the exact meaning of this distinction, all of whose philosophical implications obviously cannot be discussed here.

"Plato very well realized"—as the *Critique of Pure Reason* points out—"that our faculty of knowledge feels a much higher need than merely to spell out appearances according to a synthetic unity in order to be able to read them as experience. He knew that our reason naturally exalts itself to modes of knowledge which so far transcend the bounds of experience that no given empirical object can ever coincide with them, but which must nonetheless be recognized as having their own reality, and which are by no means mere fictions of the brain." [31] For Kant, the republican constitution is such an idea. [32] The first question that surely then arises is of course how an idea to which nothing real corresponds can still have reality and not be a phantasm. According to the text quoted, "our faculty of knowledge" takes two forms:

—On the one hand, as *scientific* knowledge of the object of experience, the faculty of knowledge uses rules or *concepts* to make intelligible an ever-increasing number of empirically observable sensory phenomena. In this way, which is clearly that of the *understanding,* our knowledge is properly limited to the two conditions that mark our finitude, space and time: it does not seek to get beyond these frameworks to think of "supernatural" (extratemporal and extraspatial) hypothetical entities.

—On the other hand, however, according to the complex mechanism whose analysis we shall ignore here, [33] human thought cannot stop overstepping the limits of scientific knowledge: it then tries to rise to the contemplation of entities (God, the soul, or, in this case, the republican constitution) that are by definition nonvisible in experience for they are nonsensory, extraspatial, and extratemporal. This being so, *reason* (and not the understanding) produces *Ideas* (and not concepts) whose objective reality remains essentially problematic.

Thus, the Ideas of reason have a twofold status, one illusory, the other legitimate or, as Kant says, nonchimerical: the illusion lies in believing that the Ideas, like simple scientific concepts, could have their objective truth in experience. To limit ourselves to a telling example: this is what takes place when one claims to detect in the real world signs (the beauty of the universe, the perfection of a particular natural being, and so forth) that would empirically prove the existence of God, or when one believes it possible to realize here and now a perfect political constitution and thus to create a wholly rational society. It does not follow, however, that the Ideas, for want of being embodiable in their totality, are entirely doomed to illusion. Correctly thought of, they indicate an ideal or, if you will, a regulative principle for thinking about the world. To take up the same examples again: as a principle of reflection the Idea of God—that is, on the theoretical level, the Idea of an omniscient being—continues to stimulate the intellectual activity of even the least metaphysical and most atheistic thinkers—complete knowledge of the world certainly being just an "Idea," a humanly unattainable ideal, yet one that guides, knowingly or not, the search of someone attempting to advance knowledge in any scientific domain. Similarly, the Idea of a free, rational, and just society in which law would reign absolutely, in other words, the republican Idea, although plainly *empty,* continues to impel those whom we call "moral beings" or "men of good will," serving them as both a signpost and a criterion for judging positive (historical) reality.

The republican Idea, whose ideal type we can deduce out of its historical manifestation in France during the second half of the nineteenth century, explicitly presents itself, through the notion of participation rights, as (*a*) a *synthesis* that is both (*b*) *humanistic* and (*c*) *antihistoricist* of the antinomy at the core of the history of human rights (permissions and entitlements). These three elements can easily be conceived of as indissolubly linked when we think of them as based on the distinction between understanding and reason.

(*a*) The antinomy of permissions and entitlements can be philosophically described as stemming from a confusion of the political understanding and political reason:[34]

—To be legitimate, the liberal thesis should be limited to *defending the viewpoint of understanding about right,* as does Tocqueville's argument against the inscription of the right to work in the constitution. It is clear, and liberalism should be granted this point, that entitlements, which express the need for social justice on the legal level, cannot ever be anything other than an Idea of reason: they cannot really belong to positive right (unless in the Soviet Constitution!), for their perfect actualization is by definition absolutely impossible; at least some of these entitlements—for example, the putative rights to health, leisure, culture, and so forth—come under the category of happiness, and happiness, meaning the complete satis-

faction of all our desires, is obviously an Idea whose exhaustive presentation is (unfortunately) excluded: if entitlements can be called
"rights," it is only in the sense of a *natural right* remaining as such
irreducibly at a distance from positive right. Liberalism, however,
goes further (the reason why a legitimate thesis lapses into error or,
more precisely, *illusion*) and positivistically *absolutizes* the viewpoint of the understanding when liberalism declares that the idea of
entitlements is absurd and chimerical because it is empty, without
seeing that they can derive from natural right and not simply, as the
liberal tradition believes, from morality (public charity).

—For its part, the *antithesis* commits the reverse and strictly
metaphysical error of making what is merely an Idea of reason a concept of the understanding: it then posits entitlements as actualizable
and even goes so far as to suspend permissions to make this actualization possible (which promises a very long heyday to the dictatorship of the proletariat, that actualization by definition representing
an endless task!). "Real socialism"—in contrast to a democratic socialism that would unambiguously think of itself under the republican Idea—then also presents the totalitarian dangers of an alleged
embodiment of what is in fact merely a metaphysical illusion.

For its part, the republican Idea clearly provides the solution to
the antinomy: it is indissolubly, but without metaphysical confusion,
a politics of the understanding (the reason why it can incorporate
liberalism) and a politics of reason (the reason why it assigns its ap-
propriate place to the socialist Idea of entitlements: that of an infinite
task or, if you will, a principle of reflection).

(*b*) The reference to this republican Idea thus also includes *a
reference to the values of modern humanism since the Enlightenment,* for it refers to the supposition that the public space—the res
publica—is *ideally* grounded on the possibility of rational communication between men. What's more, it affirms the at least de jure
unity of humanity in contrast to the barbarism that, whatever form it
takes, always amounts to thinking of humanity as *essentially* divided
(into races, classes , or even into heterogeneous cultures). In a philosophical context in which reason seems to have become "the fiercest enemy of thought," it apparently needs to be recalled that the
"right to difference" is not without ambiguities: for example, if we
think of it in the framework of an ancient, purposeful, and hierarchical cosmology, it may well mean the recognition of essential divisions within humanity, a theme whose possible political uses (slav-

ery, of which we spoke in our introduction, being merely one of many possibilities on the subject) may be hard to foresee. We are certainly not unaware that, even today, the (transcendental) presupposition that communication is always de jure possible in humanity—a permanent presupposition in the whole critical tradition up to Habermas[35] and one that in no way rules out respect for differences, but rather requires them—we are certainly not unaware that, even today, it is the target of criticisms that—the fact is not lacking in comedy—present themselves as the transcendence of hackneyed metaphysical positions and as the extreme point of the current state of philosophy. Let us put it clearly: "genealogical" criticisms of modern humanism and reason have been a commonplace of philosophy *for more than two centuries*! Such arguments are found not only in Heidegger, Nietzsche, and Kierkegaard, but also in all German romantic thinking, for example, in the remarkable critiques of idealism that we see in Jacobi or Schelling. To claim to have discovered only now the doubtful and oppressive character of the great systems or, as they say, "great narratives," that, for the first time, it is a matter of demolishing the idols of rationalist metaphysics (historical determinism, the primacy of consciousness or subjectivity, the identity claims of dogmatism, and so on) represents a program that is explained only by the penury in which French philosophy sometimes seems to be plunged. To declare, as did Michel Foucault, for example (in this he is assuredly representative of a whole generation of philosophers), that "the search for a moral form that would be acceptable to everyone—in the sense that everyone should be subject to it—seems to me catastrophic"[36] is really quite odd: if this is a criticism of moral dogmatism, the "moraline" Nietzsche speaks of, in its various forms (from Jacobin Terror to the most insidious figures of social control), the undertaking is commendable, but (1) it is in no way new (after all, Hegel was the first and possibly the most brilliant critic of moral terrorism), and especially (2) it in no way implies giving up the need for communication, about which we do not see, if we think that no one is a priori excluded, how it could forbid itself any reference to the universal. In short, on this path, the door we break down is either open wide or should be carefully shut. But if the question is really one of having done with the idea of universality, with the idea that in principle, if not in fact, a communication can be established between men concerning certain principled values, then we must agree that a renunciation is called for of any reference of the rights of humanity (which, think of them as we will, do imply a minimum of universality and subjectivity) and that, perhaps without wishing to, one thus opens another door: that of barbarism.

(c) The same difficulties are encountered today in view of the last feature synthesized by the republican Idea: antihistoricism. It is clear that the reference to human rights, as conceived of in the republican Idea, in a sense implies the recognition of the suprahistorical character of certain values. Certainly, human rights appear at a determinate historical moment, and yet, once declared, they contain a requirement of universality such that they no longer seem reducible to history. Here again, because this assertion *seems* naïvely metaphysical, it clashes head-on with the deeply historicist presuppositions of certain dominant currents of French thought for which the point is to show that all our sentiments, all our beliefs, "and particularly those that seem to us the noblest and most disinterested, have a history" and as such must be the object of "genealogical" analysis.[37] Whether under the aegis of Marxism, or *on the contrary* (for here again an antinomy is involved) of that Nietzscheanism and Heideggerianism that so much intellectually marked the 1960s in France, historical relativism has become, at least until recently, a sure value, the sign, as it were, that one was "alerted" by a reiterated practice of "suspicion." Here is not the place to review the antinomies of this historicism.[38] Let us merely say that the sentiment of universality, thus in a sense of ahistoricity elicited by human rights, or by at least some of them, is a literally uncircumventable fact of consciousness, and it is without any doubt preferable to seek to understand it (if not to explain it) rather than to try fiercely, and unsuccessfully moreover, to exterminate it. We shall spare ourselves the trouble of examples concerning racism, torture, and the like, that would show this transcendence of the idea of human rights in relation to history. Here it is necessary to give place to self-reflection about matters of conscience and not of proof.

NOTES

INTRODUCTION

1. Marcel Gauchet, "Les Droits de l'homme ne sont pas une politique," *Le Débat,* July–August 1980.

2. Claude Lefort, "Politics and Human Rights," trans. Alan Sheridan, in *The Political Forms of Modern Society: Bureaucracy, Democracy, Totalitarianism* (Cambridge: MIT Press, 1986).

3. See the March 1980 issue of *Esprit:* Paul Thibaux, "Droit et politique," 239–72.

4. Lefort, "Politics and Human Rights."

5. It is on this basis that there appeared many analyses of the "Polish challenge" (Paul Thibaud, *Esprit,* January 1981), of the "Polish example" (Krzysztof Pomian, in *Le Débat,* February 1981), or in the "Polish breach" (*Autogestion,* February 1981) to reveal the specificity of the *juridical* demand in the name of the "rights of life that cannot be alienated." See the important issue of *Esprit* (March 1980) on the theme "Droit et politique."

6. Gauchet, "Les Droits de l'homme ne sont pas une politique."

7. P. Thibaud, "Droit et société," *Esprit* (March 1983): 85–90 (reply to our text, in the same issue, "Penser les droits de l'homme").

8. Thibaud, "Droit et politique," 3ff.

9. Thibaud, "Droit et société," 85–88.

10. Here we are thinking, of course, of both Hannah Arendt's and Michel Villey's; see above.

11. Lefort, "Politics and Human Rights."

12. Alain Duhamel, *Le Monde,* 8–9 May 1983.

13. Olivier Duhamel, "L'Évolution des dissensus français," in SOFRES, *Opinion publique enquête et commentaires* (Paris: Gallimard, 1984), 133–49. See also Alain Duhamel, Olivier Duhamel, and Jérome Jaffré, "Ce qui divise les Français," *Le Débat,* May 1984.

14. Especially if, among the 70 percent of the persons supporting freedom to unionize, we include the 40 percent who would judge their suppression "very serious" and the 30 percent who would judge it only "rather serious."

15. See also the support for social security, for which the difference is a mere eleven points (article 22 of the Universal Declaration of Human Rights of 1948: "Every person, as a member of the society, has the right to social security").

16. Article 6 of the Declaration of 1789 merely proclaims the right of all citizens to

"participate personally, or through their representatives, in the formation of the law"; on the other hand, we read in the Universal Declaration of 1948, article 21, paragraph 3: "The will of the people is the basis for the authority of the public powers; this should find expression in honest elections which should take place regularly, under universal equal suffrage and secret vote or following an equivalent procedure which assures the liberty of the vote."

17. See Jean Rivero, *Les Libertés publiques, 1: Les Droits de l'homme,* 3d ed. (Paris: Presses Universitaires de France, 1981), 104ff.

18. In its preamble, the Constitution of 4 October 1958 proclaims the support of the French people "to human rights ... as defined by the Declaration of 1789, confirmed and completed the preamble of the Constitution of 1946."

19. Lefort, "Politics and Human Rights," 255.

20. Claude Lefort, *L'Invention démocratique: Les Limites de la domination totalitaire.* (Paris: Fayard, 1981), p. 29.

21. *Nouvel Observateur,* 24 February 1984.

22. The Constitution of Year X (in fact, two "Senate consultations" of August 1802) is the one that organized Napoléon's consular dictatorship; it established electoral colleges that in each *département* include the six hundred most heavily taxed citizens.

23. This formula is that of article 6 of the Declaration of 1789; it is repeated in that of 1793: "each citizen has an *equal* right to participate in the creation of the law and in the nomination of his mandatories or agents" (article 29); the Declaration of 1795 states that "each citizen has an *equal* right to participate, immediately or mediately, in the creation of the law, in the nomination of the people's representatives and public servants" (article 20).

24. See Philippe Raynaud, "Un Romantique libéral, Benjamin Constant," *Esprit,* March 1983.

25. See chapter 4 of this book.

26. See Pierre Ronsanvallon, *La Crise de l'Etat-Providence* (Paris: Seuil, 1981), pt. 2.

27. On historicism's negation of right, see Luc Ferry and Alain Renaut, "Penser les droits de l'homme," *Esprit,* March 1983; Luc Ferry, *Political Philosophy 1: Rights—The New Quarrel between the Ancients and the Moderns,* trans. Franklin Philip (Chicago: University of Chicago Press, 1990).

28. See Hannah Arendt, *The Origins of Totalitarianism* (New York: Harcourt, Brace, 1951).

29. Jean Lacouture, *Léon Blum,* trans. George Holoch (New York: Holmes and Meier, 1982), 138. See Michel Rocard, *Parler vrai* (Paris: Seuil, 1979), 54: "It was not only communists who made mistakes in history. I am thinking of the concept of the dictatorship of the proletariat that Léon Blum continued to use, including his speech at Tours."

30. See Blum's final article, "Grande-Bretagne travailliste and Russie totalitaire," *Le Populaire-Dimanche,* 5 March 1950: Soviet Russia, "enormous country ... in which all basic personal freedoms" are "implacably rejected."

31. See Nicole Racine, "Les Socialistes français devant le régime soviétique (1920–1939)," in *Les Interprétations du stalinisme,* ed. Evelyne Pisier (Paris: Presses Universitaires de France, 1983).

32. See Lefort, "L'impensé de l'Union de la Gauche," in *L'Invention démocratique* 129ff.

33. Racine, "Les Socialistes français," 106.

34. It was not so long ago that a deputy of the majority elected in 1981 declared at the congressional podium, in addressing the opposition: "You are juridically wrong, since you are politically in the minority."

35. For a more detailed analysis, see Rivero, *Les Libertés publiques, 1*. On the distinction between permissions and entitlements, see also Raymond Aron, "Pensée sociologique et droits de l'homme," in his *Etudes politiques* (Paris: Gallimard, 1972), 216ff.

36. See the preamble of the Constitution of 1848, VIII: the republic "must, through fraternal assistance, ensure the existence of its needy citizens, by either obtaining work for them within the limits of its resources, or, in case of failure to do so by the family, by giving help to those who are not in a condition to work."

37. The formula retained in article 13 is broadly in retreat in relation to a genuine proclamation of the right to work: "the *freedom* to work" is guaranteed, and society limits itself to *encouraging* "the development of work through free elementary schooling, professional education . . . and the establishment of public works such as to employ idle hands."

38. The constitutional plan written by the first Constituent Assembly, elected in October 1945, by a left majority, was even clearer (it was rejected in the referendum of 5 May 1946, only the socialists and communists campaigning for the "yes" vote; it opened to a Declaration of the Rights of Man that grouped rights under two titles: (1) freedoms; (2) social and economic rights. The duality is thus made explicit. On the other dispositions concerning human rights in the Western constitution after 1945, see Rivero, *Les Libertés publiques*, 1:101–2.

39. See especially Michel Villey, *Le Droit et les droits de l'homme* (Paris: Presses Universitaires de France, 1983). We come back in part 1 to the principle and horizon of this criticism of the discourse of human rights.

40. Here is the *principle* of the proliferation recorded by Villey; entitlements are indeed strictly relative to the degree of overall material abundance attained by the society considered: see Raymond Aron, *Essai sur les libertés* (Paris: Calmann-Lévy, 1977), 116ff.

41. The preamble to the Declaration of Independence proclaims that "all men are created equal" and "are endowed by their Creator with certain inalienable rights," including "life, liberty, and the pursuit of happiness."

42. See the turn-of-the-century debate between the German jurist Jellinek, advocate of a direct filiation between the American declarations (themselves held to be inherited from Lutheranism and hence Germanic culture) and the French declarations, and the French jurist E. Boutmy, defender of the radical originality of the French texts.

43. See Rivero, *Les Libertés publiques*, 1:56.

44. We use Rivero's expression; ibid., 57.

45. See Jürgen Habermas, "Natural Law and Revolution," in *Theory and Practice*, trans. John Viertel (Boston: Beacon Press, 1973), 82–120.

46. Thomas Paine, *Common Sense: The Rights of Man and Other Essential Writing* (New York: New American Library, 1984).

47. See Habermas, "Natural Law and Revolution," 93ff.

48. Ibid., 112.

49. See Luc Ferry and Evelyne Pisier-Kouchner, "Les Droits de l'homme dans les sociétés contemporaines," in *Encyclopaedia Universalis* (Paris, 1985).

50. Hannah Arendt, *On Revolution* (New York: Viking Press, 1963).

51. Supporting the idea that the guarantee of political rights (by a minimal state) is nothing without the bringing about of social rights (by an interventionist state), the mechanism of interference is clear: the defenders of entitlements will, in principle, conceive of the actualization of the declarations of human rights according to a *political* model (from high to low); similarly, in principle, the defenders of permissions alone will rely, to reject taking responsibility by the state for social rights, on the conviction that the simple guarantee of formal rights allows for the self-deployment of a social harmony through which the social rights are actualized by themselves. We come back to the modality of this slip and how, from the two sides, the coherence of the positions is not without confusion.

52. Habermas, *Theory and Practice,* 105.

53. See Ferry, *Political Philosophy 2: The System of Philosophies of History,* trans. Franklin Philip (Chicago: University of Chicago Press, 1991), chap. 1.

54. See Habermas, *Theory and Practice,* 104.

55. See Ferry, *Political Philosophy 2,* pt. 2.

56. See François Furet, "Au centre de nos préoccupations politiques," *Esprit,* September 1976.

57. For example, see Hegel, *The Difference between Fichte's and Schelling's System of Philosophy,* trans. H. S. Harris (Albany, N.Y.: State University of New York Press, 1977), 149. Hegel summarizes Fichte's position as follows: "right must be done, even though for its sake, all trust, all joy and love, all the potencies of a genuinely ethical identity, must be eradicated root and branch." Let us state that we do not take any position here on the textual accuracy of this criticism of Fichte: it is the bringing to life of the relations between political violence (terror) and ethical voluntarism that we are concerned with in Hegel's text. As for Fichte's own conception of right, see Alain Renaut, *Philosophie et droit dans la pensée de Fichte* (Paris: Presses Universitaires de France, 1985).

CHAPTER 1

1. See Thibaud, "Droit et politique," 3.

2. On the Marxist criticism of abstract right, see Alain Bergounioux and Bernard Manin, *La Social-démocratie ou le compromis* (Paris: Presses Universitaires de France, 1979), chap. 1: "Socialisme et démocratie."

3. See Ferry, *Political Philosophy 1.*

4. Historicism represents a twofold threat to the criticisms of positivity in the name of juridical norms: (1) as it implies *relativism,* it prevents any principles from appearing as a figure of the universal; (2) as *rationalist* historicism, it implies the coincidence of the ideal and the real *in* history, and hence takes away from law the role of critical authority with regard to positivity (since the split between the "is" and the "ought" loses all meaning).

5. On the reference to Merleau-Ponty, see in particular Claude Lefort, *Sur une colonne absente* (Paris: Gallimard, 1978); see also the dossier compiled by *Esprit,* June 1982.

6. Max Horkheimer and Theodor Adorno, *Dialectic of Enlightenment,* trans. John Cumming (New York: Continuum, 1972), xi.

7. Ibid., 3.

8. We must point out all the same that this was not the gesture of the Frankfurt theoreticians: despite their hesitations and the options on which they were divided, neither Horkheimer nor Adorno yielded to the mirage of a return to the ancients (if only to the extent that, wrongly or rightly, the *Dialectic of Enlightenment* seemed to them to already appear in the *Odyssey;* see also Horkheimer and Adorno, *Dialectic of Enlightenment,* 44ff.

9. For the writings of Michel Villey, see particularly *La Formation de la pensée juridique moderne* (Paris: Montchrétien, 1975); idem, *Philosophie du droit* (Paris: Dalloz, 1978). Further on, we indicate his contributions to the debate about human rights.

10. See particularly Villey, *La Formation de la pensée juridique moderne,* 24ff.

11. See the Aristotelian notion of "equity" defined as the principle in the name of which should be effected a process of rectification or balance in contrast to a simple mechanical application of written laws (*Nicomachean Ethics,* V, 14).

12. For a more detailed analysis, the reader is referred to Alexandre Koyré, *From the Closed World to the Infinite Universe* (Baltimore: Johns Hopkins University Press, 1957); on the philosophical significance of this representation of the Greek world, see Heidegger's *What Is a Thing?* trans. W. B. Barton, Jr., and Vera Deutsch (Chicago: Henry Regnery, 1967).

13. See of course Descartes's theory of movement in his *Principles of Philosophy,* book 2.

14. On this point see Aristotle, *Physics* IV, particularly 211 a 5ff.

15. On the definition of right as the science of distribution, see the writings of Michel Villey, for example, "Une Définition du droit," in *Seize Essais de philosophie du droit* (Paris: Dalloz, 1969); see also *NRH,* chap. 4.

16. See Villey, *Philosophie du droit,* 2:32–84; see also, despite some differences in nuance, the work of the Brussels school, particularly that of Chaim Perelman, showing that Aristotle's analysis of the rationality of right is found in the *Topics* and not the *Analytics.*

17. This obvious effect of historicism is clearly attacked by Fichte in the *Contributions* of 1793: "We would ... look to success as the touchstone of both justice and wisdom and then, once arrived, call the robber a hero or a criminal, and Socrates either an offender or a virtuous sage?" We should recall in passing that modernity is sometimes capable of denouncing the antijuridical effects of historicism.

18. Here we repeat Pierre Aubenque's analysis in "La Loi chez Aristote," in *Archives de philosophie du droit* (Paris: Sirey, 1980).

19. See, for example, Lefort, "Politics and Human Rights," 239, where Strauss is hailed as "one of the most penetrating thinkers of our time," whose writings "prepared the way" for thinking about the possible foundation of human rights.

20. Leo Strauss, "What Is Political Philosophy?" in *"What Is Political Philosophy?" and Other Studies* (Glencoe, Ill.: Free Press, 1959), 27.

21. Plato, *The Republic* IV, 434 c (Paul Shorey trans.). On this point see Y.-P. Thomas, "Politique de droit chez Platon, la nature du juste," in *Archives de philosophie du droit* 16:87ff.

22. Villey's most important criticisms are collected in *Le Droit et les droits de l'homme.*

23. Villey, *Philosophie du droit,* 2:81–104.

24. Ibid., 99.

25. Ibid.

26. Aubenque, "La Loi chez Aristote," 157.

27. See Villey, *Seize Essais de philosophie du droit,* 140–233. On this theme in Strauss, see, for example, in *NRH* 166ff, the analysis of the birth of modern natural right in Hobbes (the deduction of natural law from the desire for self-preservation).

28. On the historical pinpointing of this break, see Villey, *La Formation de la pensée juridique moderne,* 199ff.

29. We note in passing that, stressing that the modern definition of natural rights proceeds from individual wills, Strauss cites Edmund Burke: "The little catechism of the rights of men is soon learned; and the inferences are in the passions." The reactivation of ancient natural right thus leads, significantly, to repeating arguments used by one of the most dedicated opponents of human rights. On this return to Burke, see also Villey, *Philosophie du droit,* 1:161; see also, infra, our earlier analysis of the pages Hannah Arendt devotes to Burke's critique.

30. We find the same idea in Strauss in the form of a criticism of Rousseau: "If the ultimate criterion of justice becomes the general will, i.e., the will of a free society, cannibalism is as just as its opposite. Every institution hallowed by a folk-mind has to be regarded as sacred" ("What Is Political Philosophy?" 51).

31. Villey, "L'Humanisme et le droit," in *Seize Essais,* 60.

32. Villey, *Le Droit et les droits de l'homme,* 8–9: apparently, human rights, opposable to the state and its laws, serve as a brake to the identification of the just and positive right; however, as the reference to these rights is inscribed in the horizon of subjective right, it also shares in the movement that leads to positivism.

33. A further reason for not caricaturing Villey's position: this is a *juridical* antihumanism, his criticism of humanism being strictly limited to the supposedly antijuridical effects of the installation of man as the source and end of right; but this criticism can coexist with the recognition of the *ethical* value of humanism (see *Seize Essais,* 70): Villey's main criticism of the discourse of human rights is thus of confounding *right* and *morality*—and one cannot, de facto, be unaware of the risks of this confusion. One of the tasks bequeathed to us by Villey's criticism will thus be to spell out the status of the reference to human rights: if human rights are not a politics, are they law to any greater degree?

34. Lefort, "Politics and Human Rights," 66.

35. Gauchet, "Les Droits de l'homme ne sont pas une politique," 4. See also Lefort, "Politics and Human Rights," 257: "With less talent [than Joseph de Maistre or Marx] a number of our contemporaries continue to sneer at abstract humanism." Permit us not to name them here.

36. On Heidegger's analysis of "the metaphysics of subjectivity," see Ferry, *Political Philosophy 1,* 7ff.

37. On this point, see Ferry, *Political Philosophy 1.*

38. See Heidegger, "Letter on Humanism," trans. Frank A. Capuzzi and J. Glenn Gray, in *Martin Heidegger: Basic Writings* (New York: Harper and Row, 1977), 224. On this point see Luc Ferry and Alain Renaut, "La Dimension éthique dans la pensée de Heidegger," in Ute Guzzoni, ed., *Nachdenken über Heidegger* (Hildesheim: Gerstenberg, 1980), incorporated in Ferry, *Political Philosophy 2,* and "La Question de l'éthique après Heidegger," in *Les Fins de l'homme* (Paris: Galilée, 1981).

39. See, for example, Hannah Arendt, *The Life of the Mind,* vol. 1: *Thinking* (New York: Harcourt Brace Jovanovich, 1977), 212: "I have clearly joined the ranks of those who for some time now have been attempting to dismantle metaphysics, and philoso-

phy with all its categories, as we have known them from their beginning in Greece until today."

40. Hannah Arendt, *Imperialism* (San Diego: Harcourt Brace Jovanovich, 1979), 170.

41. Ibid., 179.

42. Ibid.

43. See Ferry, *Political Philosophy 1,* 9ff.

44. Arendt, *Imperialism,* 179. This recognition of what is "irrefutable" in Burke's criticism does not exclude, for Arendt, a distancing, in other respects, with regard to a dimension of nationalism found in his *Reflections on the Revolution in France* (see Arendt, *Imperialism,* 109–11).

45. Arendt, *Imperialism,* 177.

46. Ibid., 179.

47. See Ferry, *Political Philosophy 1.*

48. See Fichte's criticisms of the metaphysical illusions on the subject (Ferry, *Political Philosophy 1,* 73ff).

49. In many respects, Fichte's 1796 *Basis of Natural Right* represents an attempt, using his criticism of metaphysics as a basis, to make clear the political import of this discourse about human rights (understood as "the right of each to see his rights recognized").

50. See also Ferry, "De la critique de l'historicisme à la question du droit," in *Rejouer le politique* (Paris: Galilée, 1981).

51. Aubenque, "La Loi chez Aristote," 157.

52. Villey, "L'Humanisme et le droit," 64.

53. For example, see Villey, *Le Droit et les droits de l'homme.*

54. Heidegger, "The Anaximander Fragment," in *Early Greek Thinking,* trans. David Farrell Krell and Frank A. Capuzzi (New York: Harper and Row, 1975), 43ff.

CHAPTER 2

1. We are well aware that any generalization is by definition exposed to objections of exceptions and counterexamples: thus it is clear that Machiavelli or the legists of the end of the sixteenth century are not taken into account in the typology we sketch here (although they already establish a break with ancient thought and in this way set the stage for the advent of the school of *jus naturale*). It is also clear that a writer like Montesquieu is quite hard to situate within modernity. These remarks do not in any way cast doubt for us on the fact that modern thought predominantly takes first the form of natural right, then that of the political theory of the relations between state and society.

2. On Hobbes as the founder of modern artificialism, see Pierre Manent's excellent *La Naissance de le politique moderne* (Paris: Payot, 1979).

3. The doctrine of individual rights that is at the origin of the declarations of the rights of man already appears in the first absolutist theoreticians of limited sovereignty. See Blandine Barret-Kriegel, *L'Etat et les esclaves* (Paris: Seuil, 1979), chap. 3.

4. In Robert Derathé, *Jean-Jacques Rousseau et la science politique de son temps* (Paris: Vrin, 1948), which here remains the work of reference.

5. See ibid., 248ff.

6. It goes without saying that self-determination does not consist in doing everything one wants, but that it gets its full meaning only in the notion of autonomy as Rousseau and Kant think of it.

7. Derathé, *Jean-Jacques Rousseau,* 260.

8. See Rousseau's *Discourse on the Origin of Inequality;* this is the sense of Rousseau's criticism of the alleged right that an individual (or people) would have to go "freely" into slavery.

9. See Rousseau's *Geneva Manuscript,* bk. 1, chap. 5, and *SC,* bk. 1, chap. 5, and especially bk. 3, chap. 16.

10. Derathé, *Jean-Jacques Rousseau,* 292.

11. See Léon Duguit, *Souveraineté et liberté* (Paris: Alcan, 1922), 81 (quoted by Derathé in *Jean-Jacques Rousseau,* 293).

12. See Alexis Philonenko, *Jean-Jacques Rousseau et la pensée du malheur* (Paris: Vrin, 1984).

13. "For a will to be general, it is not always necessary that it be unanimous, but it is necessary that all votes be counted; any formal exclusion ruptures the generality" (bk. 2, chap. 2, note).

14. Gottfried Wilhelm Leibniz, *Leibniz; Selections* (New York: Charles Scribner's Sons, 1951), § 57.

15. Philonenko, *Jean-Jacques Rousseau et la pensée du malheur,* 31–32.

16. Fichte—of whom we know that Philonenko is presently the leading specialist—is to our knowledge the lone great philosopher to have a good understanding of the monadological structure of the general will as is shown in this text taken from *Science of Rights.* The difference between the general will and the will of all, writes Fichte, "is not at all impossible to understand. Each individual wishes to keep for himself and to give away as little as possible; but, since these wills are in conflict, the contradictory element is suppressed and what remains as end result is that each should have what is proper to him. When we envision two persons in some sort of commerce with each other, we can always suppose that each one wants to get the better of the other. But since neither one wishes to lose, that part of their will cancels itself out reciprocally, and their common will consists in each obtaining his just part" (*Grundlage des Naturrechts,* in *Sämtliche Werke* 3:106–7).

17. Philonenko, *Jean-Jacques Rousseau et la pensée du malheur,* 34. Let us stress that to refuse, as Rousseau does, the existence of political parties in the legislative assembly does not have a flatly "totalitarian" sense. Witness the fact that the defenders of the liberal theory of national representation, in particular Sieyès, back up Rousseau on this point. We return to this matter further on.

18. Ibid., 38.

19. It is in other words a problem of "schematization" in Kant's sense, as Philonenko suggests.

20. See Philonenko, *Jean-Jacques Rousseau et la pensée du malheur,* chap. 3: "Finitude et politique."

21. Quoted and discussed by Philonenko, ibid., 49ff. We can say in this sense that "the theory of the legislator ... is Jean-Jacques's desperate effort to smooth out the apparently insurmountable difficulties born of the inadequacy of any form of government, excepting the defunct direct democracy" (p. 565)

22. Which would presuppose a "wickedness" of the people.

23. Giving it content would entail that politics be a *celebration* while it is merely

the *theater* of our finitude. On the notion of celebration, see Jean Starobinski, *La Transparence et l'obstacle* (Paris: Gallimard, 1971).

24. M. Gauchet, "Preface," in Benjamin Constant, *Ecrits politique* (Paris: Livre de Poche, LGF, 1980).

25. In the eyes of most liberals of the time, the Jacobin Terror of 1793 seemed a throwback, a return to the ancien régime in modernity. See the fine studies of François Furet on Edgar Quinet, particularly "Quinet et Tocqueville," *Commentaire,* no. 26, 1984.

26. Although it is clearly present in some fashion in the whole liberal tradition prior to Sieyès and Constant, and also formulated within the framework of German philosophy, by Kant and, in a very different mode, by Hegel (see infra).

27. As Gauchet shows, this passage is also one from a political temporality organized on the basis of the past, to a political temporality organized on the basis of the present.

28. Which implies a temporality organized on the basis of the future.

29. Historicism is philosophically the ultimate basis of this antivoluntarist representation of the social common to the whole liberal tradition.

30. Marcel Gauchet, "Introduction," in Constant, *Ecrits politiques,* 67.

31. Ibid., 71ff., in which Gauchet suggests how this increase in fact corresponds not to the addition of a principle external to liberalism (for example, to the requirements of socialism), but to the necessity, in face of the increasing autonomization of the social, of developing a place (the state) where it can be as it were recuperated, represented, and controlled. It thus is not a zero-sum game: the state does not necessarily grow at the expense of the civil society and vice versa. Both can grow together.

32. See the *Untersuchungen über die Französische Revolution* of 1792. See also Philonenko, *Jean-Jacques Rousseau et la pensée du malheur,* 3, 34.

33. See Derathé, *Jean-Jacques Rousseau,* 260ff.

34. Here we follow the noteworthy analysis of Carré de Malberg. See *Contribution à la théorie générale de l'Etat,* 1922 (reprint; Paris: Centre Nationale de Recherches Scientifiques, 1962), 2:212ff.

35. The doctrine of national representation so well separates election from representation that the king himself, though not elected, can be part of the representatives as he participates, if only by his right of veto, in the development of the national will.

36. See *Archives parlementaires,* first series, 8: 581ff., a debate discussed by Malberg, *Contribution à la théorie générale de l'Etat,* 253ff.

37. "For if these great bodies could be constituted in such a way as to move easily, delegates would be useless. I even say they would be dangerous."

38. Malberg, *Contribution à la théorie générale de l'Etat,* 235.

39. This division is to be understood only de facto and not de jure, for, on the one hand, it "suffices" to become a landowner to go from the passive to the active, and on the other hand, the representatives represent the nation as a whole, and not this or that category.

40. See Hannah Arendt, *Lectures on Kant's Political Philosophy* (Chicago: University of Chicago Press, 1982). An exception—usual, it is true, in this tradition of blindness: that of Philonenko who devotes a remarkable introduction to the French translation of the *Doctrine of Right.*

41. Here is the place to recall, in order to avoid a misunderstanding, that it is obviously Hegel and not Kant who first introduced the notion of civil society and state in

the philosophical vocabulary. Like most writers of the school of natural right, Kant was content to contrast "natural society" (*natürliche Gesellschaft*) with civil society (*bürgerliche Gesellschaft*) to designate what we would now call the society and the state. There is a good deal of work—unfortunately eluded by most studies of Hegel's philosophy of right—yet to be done to analyze the way in which the *Philosophy of Right* repeats and considerably modifies Kant's *Doctrine of Right*. Let us say here, where it is not a matter of going too far into the purely philosophical structure of these works, that this work should have as a guiding thread the idea that Hegel's philosophy of right is opposed to the metaphysics of morals, as his philosophy of nature is opposed to Kant's metaphysics of nature. If, despite these difficulties in vocabulary, we present Kant here as the true thinker of the distinction between society and state, the reason is that Hegel's opposition of the civil society and the state seems to us to correspond much less well to what we usually understand by these terms. At the very heart of the chapter on civil society, Hegel distinguishes in his philosophy of right a liberal and nearly Kantian idea of the distinction between society and state that seems in other respects to correspond more to the current sense than does Hegel's distinction itself. The Hegelian state, a synthesis of Platonism (substantial totality) and liberalism (autonomy of the social), doesn't seem to us to have any correspondent in contemporary political vocabulary. We shall formulate a hypothesis (without any certainty) to explain the paradox, that he who introduces the society-state pair in the political vocabulary does so in a now somewhat forgotten and at the very least unusual sense: Marxist criticism of Hegel's philosophy of right, suggesting the idea that the Hegelian state is merely the superstructural product of civil society (hence a false universal), leads to eventually assimilating it to the liberal state, thus in reality, to what Hegel describes in the chapter on the civil society.

42. Kant, *Groundings for the Metaphysics of Morals* (AK IV, 415), in *Immanuel Kant: Ethical Philosophy,* trans. James W. Ellington (Indianapolis: Hackett, 1983), 98.

43. For a more complete analysis, see Bernard Rousset, *La Doctrine kantienne de l'objectivité* (Paris: Vrin, 1967).

44. Obviously these expressions are not to be taken in the sense they presently have in juristic doctrine.

PART 2, PREAMBLE

1. See Raymond Aron, *Les Etapes de la pensée sociologique* (Paris: Gallimard-Tel, 1967), 275ff.

2. See Claude Nicolet, *L'Idée républicaine en France* (Paris: Gallimard, 1982), 137ff.

3. Aron, *Pensée sociologique,* 223.

CHAPTER 3

1. *OC,* vol. 8: see particularly *Les Démocrates assermentés et les réfractaires,* a pamphlet in which Proudhon advocates abstention from the elections of 1863 and summarizes his development in relation to the republicans from 1832.

2. See Proudhon's *General Idea of the Revolution in the Nineteenth Century,* trans. John Beverly Robinson (London: Freedom Press, 1923). ("Traditional negation of the government, emergence of the idea that succeeds it"). Citations are to the French *OC.*

3. See Proudhon, *Confessions d'un révolutionnaire*, chap. 20: "La Constitution sociale subalternise, nie la constitution politique."

4. Proudhon, *General Idea of Revolution*, in *OC* 2:187.

5. Proudhon, "Du Principe fédératif," in *OC* 15:330.

6. On democracy and republic see *OC*, 13:236.

7. On Proudhon's debate with Rousseau, see *OC*, 13:118ff; *General Idea of Revolution*, in *OC*, 2:189ff. See also Henri Arvon, *Les Libertariens américains: De l'anarchisme individualiste à l'anarcho-capitalisme* (Paris: Presses Universitaires de France, 1983), 28–34.

8. Here Proudhon is quoting the declaration of 3 September 1791 (*De la justice*, in *OC*, 1:410).

9. See also *OC*, 1:453: "Man therefore has rights in only an indirect way."

10. *OC*, 1:414: "That amounts to saying that through justice each of us feels himself both as person and collectivity, individual and family, citizen and people, man and humanity."

11. Proudhon's analysis is curiously reminiscent of the one done by Marx in *The Jewish Question*.

12. See also Proudhon, *What Is Property? An Enquiry into the Principle of Right and of Government*, trans. Benjamin R. Tucker (New York: Howard Fertig, 1966). Quotation from *OC* 4:299. All cites from *OC*.

13. See Proudhon, *General Idea of Revolution*, in *OC*, 2:66.

14. See Proudhon, *What Is Property?*, in *OC*, 4:310.

15. It is interesting to note that one contemporary form of hyperliberalism [in America, extreme laissez-faire conservatism—Trans.] finds its true inspiration in anarchism. See, for example, Pierre Lémieux, *Du libéralisme à l'anarcho-capitalisme* (Paris: Presses Universitaires de France, 1983).

16. We note, at the end of this analysis of Proudhon's thinking about human rights, that one can find similar themes in P. A. Kropotkin's *The Great French Revolution, 1789–1793*, trans. N. F. Dryhurst (New York: G. P. Putnam's Sons, 1909). In chapter 19, human rights are described as the "general principles" of "a profound transformation in the relation between the various levels of society"—which nevertheless requires that one go well beyond the simple "professions of democratic faith" to which the Declarations of 1776 and 1789 are limited; for to liberate humanity it is not enough to guarantee "the equality of all before the law" and "the right of the nation to give itself the government that it wants": such a restrictive interpretation of human rights would allow the "economic relations between citizens" to survive and, in addition, would not truly attack the "principle of authority." In this sense, the French Revolution, though it began "a work of emancipation" by abolishing bondage and absolute power, nevertheless remained far from the mark: a "next revolution" should, by contesting the very principle of power, complete what the Declaration of 1789, "a profession of faith in bourgeois liberalism," merely gave a hint of.

17. [Earlier Ferry cited this volume in *OC*; now he switches to another edition—Trans.]

18. See also *GIR*, 118: "all the revolutions have done nothing but reconstitute tyranny: I make no more exception for the Constitution of 1793 than for that of 1848, which are, nonetheless, the two most advanced expressions of French democracy."

19. See Pierre Ansart, *Marx et l'anarchisme: Essais sur les sociologies de Saint Simon* (Paris: Presses Universitaires de France, 1969).

20. See Alexis Philonenko, "Kant und die Ordnungen des Reelen," in *Etudes kantiennes* (Paris: Vrin, 1982).

21. The following repeats without significant changes some pages of an article written with Evelyne Pisier-Kouchner for the *Encyclopaediea Universalis* on the theme of human rights in contemporary societies.

22. See Karl Marx, "The German Ideology," in Robert Tucker, ed., *The Marx-Engels Reader* (New York: Norton, 1978), 187.

23. Habermas, *Theory and Practice,* 111.

24. See "The German Ideology," MEGA I/5:308-9.

25. Karl Marx, "On the Jewish Question," in *The Marx-Engels Reader* (New York: Norton, 1978), 42.

26. Ibid.

27. Ibid.

28. Karl Marx, "The Class Struggle in France: 1848 to 1850," trans. Robert Tucker, in Karl Marx, *Surveys from Exile: Political Writings* (New York: Random House, 1973), 2:69-70.

29. Claude Lefort, "Politics and Human Rights," *Libre* 7 (1980).

30. Ibid., 246.

31. Ibid., 248.

32. Ibid., 250.

33. Ibid., 257.

CHAPTER 4

1. For example, see Pierre Lémieux, *Du libéralisme à l'anarcho-capitalisme* (Paris: Presses Universitaires de France, 1983), chap. 5: "Redécouvrir les droits de l'homme."

2. In this regard, see Barret-Kriegel, *L'Etat et les esclaves,* 53ff., "Les Droits de l'homme."

3. On Tocqueville's activity on the constitution commission, see J.-C. Lamberti, "Tocqueville et la Constitution de 1848," *Commentaire* 25 (1984).

4. On this point see Bernard Manin's excellent "Les Deux Libéralismes: Marché ou contre-pouvoirs," *Interventions* (May-June-July 1984): 12.

5. Ibid., 14.

6. See the title of Wilhelm von Humboldt's 1792 book *The Limits of State Action* (London: Cambridge University Press, 1969).

7. Jacques Julliard, quoted in *Interventions* (May-June-July 1984): 3.

8. We admit that the Guizot text we are about to bring up is surely not the best and it in no way prevents one's taking an interest in other aspects of his work. It is still true that this dimension of his thinking is not negligible, however.

9. Julliard, quoted in *Interventions,* 3.

10. See particularly the articles of B. Manin and H. Lepage in *Commentaire* 22 (Summer 1983). We repeat ourselves here by developing our chronicle "Ni Marx, ni Hayek," *L'Ane* 17 (July–August 1984).

11. See particularly volume 1, *The Mirage of Social Justice.*

12. Friedrich A. von Hayek, *The Road to Serfdom* (Chicago: University of Chicago Press, 1944).

13. On Hayek's conception of the state, see the perfect analysis (whose critical dimension should be noted) by Raymond Aron as early as his *Essais sur les libertés* (Paris:

Calmann-Lévy, 1965), 125ff.; see also in his *Etudes politiques* (Paris: Gallimard, 1972) the two essays "La Définition libérale de la liberté" (on Hayek's *The Constitution of Liberty* [Chicago: University of Chicago Press, 1960]) and "Liberté, libérale or libertaire?"

14. *LLL,* 2:86: "The distributive justice at which socialism aims is thus irreconcilable with the rule of law." See also p. 68: "So long as the belief in 'social justice' governs political action, this process must progressively approach nearer and nearer to a totalitarian system."

15. Jacques Julliard, in *Le Nouvel Observateur,* no. 1013: "La Nouvelle Idole de la droite."

16. Ibid.

17. Nathan Glazer "Vers une société autonome," *Commentaire* 25 (1984): 66ff.

18. For the analysis of this letter, see Alain Renaut, "Marxisme et déviation stalinienne," in *Les Interpétations du stalinisme,* ed. Evelyne Pisier-Kouchner (Paris: Presses Universitaires de France, 1983).

19. On this type of difficulties, see Henri Lepage, article quoted in *Commentaire,* p. 353—without which the author sees neither the theoretical roots of the difficulties nor their insurmountability.

20. See Ferry, *Political Philosophy 2.*

21. See Philippe Raynaud, "Un Romantique libéral, Benjamin Constant," *Esprit* (March 1983), particularly pp. 61–62.

22. Benjamin Constant, *De la liberté chez les modernes: ecrits politiques* (Paris: Livre de Poche, 1980), 501.

23. See Raynaud, "Un Romantique libéral," 65.

24. Ibid., 62.

25. In Tocqueville himself, it could be shown how, for example, the progress of democracy is described as part of the plan of providence: see, for example, this passage from the introduction to *Democracy in America* (New York: Vintage Books, 1945), 1:6 (in which, once again, one is aware of the presence of the schema of the cunning of reason): "The various occurrences of national existence have everywhere turned to the advantage of democracy: all men have aided it by their exertions, both those who have intentionally labored in its cause and those who have served it unwittingly; those who have fought for it and even those who have declared themselves its opponent have all been driven along in the same direction, have all labored to one end; some unknowingly and some despite themselves, all have been blind instruments in the hands of God." In other words, "men create history without knowing the history they are creating."

CHAPTER 5

1. See Jean Jaurès, "Question de méthode," in *Oeuvres de Jean Jaurès* (Paris: Rieder, 1933), 6:241ff.

2. For a more detailed analysis, see L. Hamon, *Socialisme et pluralités* (Paris: Gallimard, 1976) and also Manin and Bergounioux, *La Social-démocratie ou le compromis.*

3. See, for example, Eduard Bernstein, *Les Présupposés du socialisme* (Paris: Seuil, 1974), 58ff.

4. In Jean Jaurès, *Discours* (Paris: Gonthier, 1964).

5. Hence Jaurès's "ministerialism" or "possibilism" in the Millerand affair.

6. Jean Jaurès, *Idéalisme et matérialisme,* in *Oeuvres,* 6:7.

7. Ibid.

8. See Jean Jaurès, *Studies in Socialism,* trans. Mildred Minturn (New York: Kraus Reprints, 1970). On this point see Alexis Philonenko's fine "Fichte et Jaurès," in *Etudes kantiennes.*

9. Jean Jaurès, *Histoire socialiste de la Révolution française* (Paris, 1922), 1:341ff.

10. See chapter 3 of this volume.

11. Jaurès, *Oeuvres,* 6:117ff.

12. Let us once again direct the reader on this point to the judicious remarks of Claude Lefort, "L'Impensé de l'Union de la Gauche," in *L'Intention démocratique* (Paris: Fayard, 1981).

13. This at a speech at the Panthéon in July 1937.

14. See Jaurès "Socialisme et république," in *Oeuvres,* vol. 6.

15. See also the fine study about this work by Philippe Raynaud, "Destin de l'idéologie républicaine."

16. The whole religious and monarchical tradition legitimated the kingdom's laws by their "oldness"; here history takes the place of the code.

17. On this text, see *IR,* 292, n. 3.

18. They are patiently reconstructed in Nicolet's book, to which we can only allude (p. 342ff.).

19. Benjamin Constant, *De la liberté des anciens,* 514.

20. He was V. Vanderwinckel (see *IR,* 343, 404).

21. It is from this angle that, as Nicolet shows (*IR,* 452ff.), the notion of "public service" elaborated by L. Duguit is rooted in the republican tradition and appears on the horizon of the affirmation, present already in 1793, that "public assistance is a sacred debt." It is in any case this filiation that the republicans themselves established (see B. Dupont-White, *L'Individu et l'etat,* 1857).

22. Pierre Laffite, *Du rôle des individus en politique,* quoted in *IR,* 191.

23. For example, the question of the election of the French president by universal suffrage divided the republic since 1848.

24. On these problems, see *IR,* 454ff.

25. See also Raynaud, "Destin de l'idéologie républicaine."

26. We can easily see why Nicolet, finding in the republican tradition what seems to him an echo of the Ciceronian conception of the republic (*IR,* 325), was less sensitive than we to this problem.

27. On this theme see Claude Lefort, *Le Travail de l'oeuvre: Machiavel* (Paris, 1972).

28. According to otherwise obviously different modalities from what they were in Rousseau (see particularly the theme of "representation"). On these differences, *IR,* 397.

29. See Raynaud, "Destin de l'idéologie républicaine," 35.

30. Among which one could count writers otherwise as different as Habermas, Aron, and even to some extent, Popper. On the Kantian infrastructure of Aron's thought in the domain of history, see the excellent work of S. Mesure, *Aron et la raison historique* (Paris: Vrin, 1984).

31. Kant, *Critique of Pure Reason,* trans. Norman Kemp Smith (London: Macmillan, 1933), 310–11.

32. See, for example, *Perpetual Peace,* article 1. It would be interesting to observe, in its opening pages, how, already for Kant, the republic is a form that implies a content;

see, for example, the link between the republican constitution and the progressive elimination of war (on this point see Alexis Philonenko, *Essais sur le philosophie de la guerre* [Paris: Vrin, 1976], 39ff.). We indicate that to our minds that Fichte's *Science of Rights* (trans. A. E. Kroeger [New York: Harper and Row, 1970]) also constitutes a presentation of the republican idea.

33. See Ferry, *Political Philosophy 2,* chap. 2; see also Ferry and Renaut, "D'un retour à Kant," *Ornicar* (Summer 1980), reprinted in *Système et critique* (Paris-Brussels: Ousia-Vrin, 1985).

34. In *Introduction à la philosophie de l'histoire* (Paris: Gallimard-Tel, 1987; first pub. 1939), 413, Raymond Aron uses the distinction between "politics of the understanding" and "politics of reason" in a sense very close to the one we give here, and sketched the possible "antinomy"—without, however, truly constructing it or describing its solution.

35. See Habermas's final elaboration of the idea of a communicational action in *Vorstudien und Ergänzungen zur Theorie des kommunicativen Handelns* (Frankfurt: Suhrkamp, 1984).

36. *Les Nouvelles,* 28 June 1984.

37. Michel Foucault, "Nietzsche, Genealogy, History," in *The Foucault Reader* (New York: Pantheon, 1984), 87.

38. See Ferry, *Political Philosophy 2,* pt. 1.

Index

INDEX

DATE DUE

DEMCO 38-296

Please remember that this is a library book,
and that it belongs only temporarily to each
person who uses it. Be considerate. Do
not write in this, or any, library book.